BUSINESS PLANS TO GAME PLANS

A Practical System for Turning Strategies into Action

Second Edition

Silver Lake Publishing
Los Angeles, California

Business Plans to Game Plans
A Practical System for Turning Strategies into Action

Second edition
Copyright © 2000 by Silver Lake Publishing

Silver Lake Publishing
2025 Hyperion Avenue
Los Angeles, California 90027

For a list of other publications or for more information, please call 1.888.663.3091. In Alaska and Hawaii and outside of the United States, please call 1.323.663.3082.

King, Jan B.
Business Plans to Game Plans—Taking Control
A practical system for turning strategies into action.
Includes index.
Pages: 362

ISBN: 1-56343-701-5
Printed in the United States of America.

Preface

To the Second Edition

During my eight years as CEO of Merritt Publishing, we faced a wide variety of challenges. I continually sought accurate data and definitive analysis. Because I initially couldn't find the diagnostic tools I needed to chart the best course for my company, I created them as I went along. These tools are included in this book to help you lead your company from your business plan through your game plan. They'll help you find the answers you need to:

☐ Write a business plan in order to redefine your company or borrow money;

☐ Create a better infrastructure to support your growth;

☐ Shift the corporate culture so employees are more accountable for their job performance;

☐ Give you better internal reporting;

☐ Determine if you need more capital, more people or new products for growth;

☐ Determine if sales are as profitable as possible; and

☐ Create and launch new products for your customers, thus maintaining competitive.

This book will also help you:

- Develop vision and mission statements;

- Set goals for your company and business plan;

- Measure your success by establishing tracking systems in the critical areas of finance, marketing, product development and operations;

- Learn by looking at what other businesses with similar challenges do; and

- Become your own consultant or know when you need outside help. You'll learn to ask the right questions, look hard at what the numbers tell you and find creative solutions to your challenges.

Growing companies tend to be confident of their technical superiority to competitors, but worry that their competitors have an edge in planning. This is especially true for small companies even though their competitors are other small businesses.

Small companies consistently operate under the fear that they are at a disadvantage when it comes to planning and operational discipline. They also tend to worry that *any* competitor comes to the game better qualified. Neither premise needs to be true. Small companies can plan and execute as well as big companies; some experts think they're even better at it.

You can be good at it, too, with the right data and a willingness to work with it. If you use the worksheets and forms in this book, you will generate enough critical data to run your business successfully.

TABLE OF CONTENTS

Business Plans to Game Plans

Business Plans to Game Plans

Introduction:
Your Game Plan

Many business books talk about business plans and strategic planning. Few tell you how to implement these plans. Why? Because the writers of business books focus on accomplishment—usually their own. They write as if once you dream the dream it magically becomes reality. They forget to write about the hard part—the work it takes to gain success.

This book focuses on the hard part, because that's what leads to success.

And make no mistake, creating and implementing a business plan takes hard work. It takes wisdom, discipline, courage, an eye for detail and—most of all—persistence. It also requires an outward focus. You must set goals, communicate them, review them, monitor their realization and stick to them when other people might abandon them.

Inventing Your Company

I know how hard these things are to do, and I know that they lead to success. In 1990, I found myself running the publishing company where I'd worked for seven years. In a matter of weeks, I had to grapple with a wide range of management problems; with little relevant experience and no formal business education, I had to learn to take control.

My company had been in business since 1957. I came to it as a writer and editor, then as the company's editorial director—a solid middle management position.

The company also had the good fortune of being so profitable and cash-rich in its formative years that there'd been little need to project or monitor sales or expenses, cash or profit. The downside of this: very little had been done to set expectations or monitor performance. It was hard to tell how well we were doing at any given time—or would do in the future.

By the time I began running the company, we were no longer cash-rich and our markets were changing dramatically, primarily due to new technologies that both made entry into our markets easier and radically changed traditional distribution methods. Without cash to invest in our own growth, I knew we would not survive over the long term.

We had no choice but to reinvent the company. We were a 40-year-old start-up. We needed a business plan and we needed a game plan.

In the months that followed, I realized that the key to our survival was getting a handle on where our cash was going and reducing our expenses. We needed to change the corporate culture from a happy family business to one where accountability played a significant role. Lastly, but most importantly, we also had to have a clear and fundamental understanding of our business—to whom we were selling products, what they would want in the future, and which of our over 200 products were profitable.

Challenge #1: Finance

Interestingly enough, it didn't occur to me in the beginning to call the CPA or glance at the financials. Instead, I asked our accounting department for a list of vendors to whom we wrote checks and a list of those checks. I wanted to know exactly where the money was going. But because the checks were listed by payee, with no notation of what was being paid for, my questions largely remained unanswered. So we used this list to get back to the record of the invoice that was being paid.

Much to the horror of the orderly accounting department, three of us transferred loads of boxes filled with old invoices from our warehouse to my office. And the manual audit began.

Company invoices resemble the bills I pay at home: we paid rent, utilities, insurance and, of course, people. I also knew that we paid for the product we produced plus its marketing. Additionally, many other items like the outside professionals, computers and miscellaneous office supplies, absorbed some of our costs.

Over several weeks, we sorted these invoices from the just-ended fiscal year into categories that seemed to make sense and covered all the types of invoices we found.

In questioning people about what each individual invoice pertained to, we found—to our amazement—that many bills were being paid for services we no longer received. This seemed particularly true for maintenance contracts on equipment we had sold years previously. Once the accounting department had been told to expect a particular bill each month, it continued to pay it without question. Many bills were addressed to accounts payable and thus paid without anyone else seeing them. We cut about $77,000 in expenses simply by questioning old invoices.

That was the first step to taking control of the business and to the development of the worksheets you will find in this book. Over time I learned to see the company as a series of five disciplines—*finance, marketing and product development, sales and customer service, operations and human resources*. I developed a system for setting up measurements and then monitoring how we performed in each area.

With regard to *finance,* I learned that the essential process involves setting projections that, in turn, allow you to monitor and manage cash, cash flow and profits—the things that keep you in business.

Marketing and product development is the great unknown to many business people; and it comes down to these questions: Who wants to buy your product and how do you find these people? How do you create new products or refine existing ones?

Sales and customer service means providing information, asking for the order and taking reorders. It centers on how easy it is for your customers to buy from your company, how easy you make it for customers to pay you, how quickly you get your product to them and how you help them when a problem arises.

Operations entails more than just maintaining plants and facilities. It involves bringing your product to market quickly and efficiently, while maintaining quality standards.

Human Resources is the traditional hiring, firing and record keeping, but it is also knowing how many people you need to efficiently run your business, knowing what to pay them and devising methods to keep morale high and turnover low.

Challenge #2: Corporate Culture

This brought me to an important question: How, exactly, could I hold the employees accountable unless I let the employees know how the company was doing?

Because my company was (at the time) partially employee-owned, the answer was to share financial information with all employees. I've heard the arguments against this kind of openness—the most compelling being that competitors can use this information against you. But I took employee ownership seriously and expected everyone at the company to help run our business. I couldn't expect others to do what I couldn't do myself— namely, run a business without knowing those numbers by which we measure success or failure. But I shared financials with my employees not for the sake of openness; rather, I did it hoping they would see how the numbers sprang from their own work. I wanted my employees to grasp the numbers as proof of their importance to the success of the company.

In short, I gave my employees access to the financials and other documents to help them make intelligent decisions about their work. I educated them about what the numbers meant in the expectation that they would use those numbers to gauge our success and guide their own action. And I discovered the remarkable power you harness by doing this. Of all the memories I have of the early years, the one I value most came after I started circulating the financials. At a rather ordinary operations meeting, an employee suggested that we reduce inventory, saying that this would increase our cash position going into the critical months of our year.

It was an extraordinary moment. Although financial consultants talk to Boards of Directors for hours about inventory accountancy, this guy—on his own—figured out that a tight inventory meant more available cash for us. He didn't earn much; indeed, fully two-thirds of my people earned more. Nonetheless, his income didn't limit his ability to comprehend the connection between inventory and cash. And his comprehension meant that my openness with the numbers had paid off.

It did not fail to register with me that when I had been a non-management employee—better paid and supposedly better informed—I had not stopped to think about the impact of inventory on cash in the bank.

Challenge #3: Marketing and Sales

It also registered that, in sharing financials, I had fundamentally changed my company. Like many entrepreneurs, the founder of my company hadn't believed in sharing financials with his employees. We received monthly sales reports, of course. And the bonus program for managers depended on profits. I knew that profits depended on sales, which interested me insofar as it pleased me to see that the books I wrote actually sold. But sales seemed magical to me; I had no way of predicting them. More to the point, I didn't think I could affect sales in any immediate way. So I eagerly awaited the accountant's proclamation at the end of each year—to find out whether I'd get a bonus. I had no clue how I could personally affect sales.

Hence, when I became CEO, starting to impact sales was hard. I took the simplest starting point I could and listed all the products we sold, from the biggest revenue earner to the least. Then I made the same list using our customer data. Eventually we were able to calculate the profitability for each product and each customer. This provided our guide to what products to sell most aggressively and to which customers. We discontinued products where we were unable to reduce costs and we raised prices where we thought the market would allow it. Some programs worked well, others didn't work at all. We closely tracked all our marketing efforts and duplicated those that worked well in tests. We constantly tested new approaches.

We also began to develop offshoots of our most successful products. We paid close attention to what our largest customers liked and didn't like and constantly improved our existing products. This resulted in a doubling of our sales in a few short years.

We worked out kinks in marketing, production and fulfillment. We refined and simplified our corporate vision and mission statements. I simplified the reports and key indicators I describe in this book, focusing them on things of importance and ridding them of everything else. Like so many other things we do, these had started out maddeningly complex, filled with all sorts of numbers and concepts. The longer I used them, the more basic they became.

When I came to the office each morning, I had to understand how the business was doing on a constantly-updated basis. Equally important, I had to make sure the other employees knew how the business was doing so that they would work toward the objectives we developed.

Challenge #4: Buying the Company

After I had been CEO for two years, the founder of the company died, leaving us without a plan for a change in ownership. The company was already 40 percent employee-owned, and we had decided together to take it to 100 percent. Some of the money had to be generated internally so we had to become more profitable. Some of the money had to be borrowed, which forced us to put together a written business and marketing plan.

Creating a goal like this one generates unbeatable motivation. Suddenly, our definition of winning was more similar to an athletic game—there was a real dollar number we had to meet or beat to win. This was the genesis of the game plans I've used. They gave employees real reasons to hold tight on expenses and develop new products—reasons that they could get excited about for their own fulfillment. Every person working at the company had a reason to step up to the plate.

An amazing thing happens when an objective becomes crystal clear. People begin to act in concert—truly, like a team. Every action becomes focused on achieving the goal.

We decided to set up a group of committees that would meet weekly and ensure the implementation of proposed plans. Two major committees monitored profitability (mostly from the revenue side) and expenses. Reporting to these committees were other subcommittees devoted to new products, customer service, strategic alliances and other business functions. I asked for volunteers to serve on the major committees, and made sure that members from each department were present.

Many of the worksheets in this book were used by our committees to monitor performance and progress toward our goal of 100 percent employee-ownership. The committees and worksheets are forms of self-measurement. They allow employees to be responsible for deciding what work needs to be done, and then for measuring what they do.

Creating Your Game Plan

I wrote this book to help other owners and managers learn what I did—but in a much shorter time. The first three chapters of the book intends to help you consider tactics and set direction and budgets. The last five chapters help you track finance, marketing and product development, sales and customer service, operations and human resources.

Each chapter (beginning with Chapter 2) starts with a discussion of relevant concepts and issues, including case studies. The case studies in each chapter make the point that none of these disciplines functions alone—all are interrelated. In times of great opportunity and growth, as well as times of business downturns and consolidation, solutions to problems come from all segments of your business working together. You will discover the need for all employees to see results in every area of your business, and not just those that directly relate to them.

A series of progressive worksheets follows each chapter's discussion. The worksheets are complete with directions on how to use them and questions related to your collected data. These exercises will help you discover your strengths and weaknesses.

In the appendices you will find how to organize the worksheets if you intend to use them for business plans or as an internal communications tool. A list of resources both in printed form and on the Internet is also included.

These worksheets are intended to be used. Please copy them freely. Distribute them to as many employees as you think useful. You may want to find them on our Web site at **bizplanstogameplans.com** and use them to input your own data on your computer. Whatever medium you use, the object of these worksheets remains the same: To help you develop your business plan and your game plan, and finally, to help you take control of your business.

CHAPTER 1:

STRATEGY AND TACTICS

Business plans, by financial necessity, must set a broad target for the success of a company without knowing the mechanics of day-to-day work or what practical challenges will emerge. You need to find tools that apply management theory and your business plan targets to the practical challenges of running a company.

Whatever your goal, defining it in a business plan is an exciting step; and because you care about that goal, your business plan looks beautiful when you initially put it together. Then you start your business and the real world intrudes. You discover that things don't play out as you imagined. You discover, in other words, the subject of this book: the difference between the business plan and the game plan—the difference between ends and means. You discover the necessity of adjusting the means by which you keep your operation headed toward its goals.

Game plans grow out of the business plans, but they need some coaxing. You get from one to the other by gradually bridging the gap and bringing into focus those things you must do to reach your goal. This chapter will take you through the focusing process. Its worksheets and exercises cover items that, by discovering the specific things your company must do to succeed, turn the abstract into the concrete.

Note the progression. You set strategy in your business plan and tactics in your game plan. You get from one to the other—from the theoretical to the practical—by monitoring and managing.

The Obvious Sports Analogy

Every coach knows that you don't win games in the locker room drawing up beautiful plays. You win games on the field, where people execute your plays—sometimes not so beautifully.

But on the field beauty doesn't matter as much as the score. You win if you know what it takes to win and then execute. In a game, this means outscoring your opponent. In business, it means many things: making money, dominating markets, providing products and services of value, making a contribution to society and giving others the opportunity to achieve success and security.

Does a coach call the next play without knowing where the ball is located on the field? No more than you can make a good marketing decision without knowing how your product sells now.

Similarly, you must know where and how the actual experience of your company deviates from the projections in your business plan—financially, in your marketing and sales efforts, operationally and in your product development efforts. You must know where you are in order to get where you want to be—before time runs out in the game.

Most business books are like cheerleaders; they offer support but little direct help when it comes to winning the game of business. You can draw energy from dreaming about your $50 million or $100 million or $1 billion company someday, but you can distract yourself, too. Whether you get that far depends on how well you plan and execute. In business as in sports, planning and executing are everything.

To do this you need both a business plan and a game plan.

Business Plans Are Integral to the Success of the Game Plan

According to a survey commissioned by AT&T in 1993, fewer than 42 percent of small businesses started operations with formal business plans.

Among businesses with revenues under $500,000, only one in three began with a formal plan.

Among small companies with written business plans, 40 percent found their projections so optimistic as to be useless once they commenced operations. Most of the others discovered their plans so incomplete as to be ineffective. Only two of three used balance sheets or profit analyses in their plans. Fewer still listed the products and services they offered or pricing information. Benchmarks like cash flow, advertising and promotional spending and capital expenses showed up rarely, if at all.

Two in three small companies found their plans lacking because the plans didn't consider the factors most important to running a growth company: finance, marketing, product development and operations.

Many small business owners in the survey attributed their success to investments in technology, employee training or marketing and not to any business plan. However, among small businesses that experienced growth over two years, 59 percent based operations on a formal plan. Of these, 70 percent attributed their success primarily to this connection.

A Greater Prosperity

Clearly, few small businesses focus on long-term planning and, more important, implementing their plans. If they did, they would likely enjoy a greater prosperity. As the AT&T survey concluded:

A specific example of the benefit of planning by small businesses is the increased accuracy of financial projections. Accurately predicting income allows small businesses to create realistic and achievable programs for growth and expansion.

As the owner or manager of a company, you probably work alone to set strategy. You know your company and its business better than anyone else. You think about your business a lot. You have a clear vision for your company and you live it. But when you step out of your office, you meet people who may not share your vision. These people may fail to execute. Your vision may falter.

Without a plan, you may falter, because it's hard to make good decisions without a good framework.

Business plans, as a rule, don't address critical issues like communicating your goals to employees and customers. They formulate broad goals, but they don't tell you how to set your business up and run it day to day so as to reach your goals. They don't tell you how to implement your business plan and measure your performance. They serve the needs of a different audience—bankers and investors. They don't help the day-to-day players who execute your game plan—coworkers, customers and vendors.

If your business plan isn't on target, you won't get financing. That's an unfortunate loss of opportunity. But if your game plan doesn't work, your company might fail after it has started. You'll end up losing a lot of money—your own and that of your investors.

The Guiding Principles

In addition to the skills I learned in developing a business plan and a game plan for my company, I also discovered that several underlying principles emerged as I put these plans into practice. The success of the plan depends upon how well your leadership solves the everyday problems. As strongly as I believe in the power of the worksheets in this book, I believe it takes your human intervention to be successful in business.

As you fill in the worksheets provided and analyze the information you find, keep in mind the following (first for your business plan, and later, for your game plan):

➡ **Set standards and give your employees the tools to meet your goals.**

Most employees feel responsible for meeting the objectives of their companies. They like their goals simple and measurable. They also meet their goals when they have the tools to do so.

As their leader, you decide what's important and communicate this to your employees. Make sure they understand your thinking; talk about what's important—a lot. Set goals and give your employees the tools they need to meet them.

You must also give your employees clear ways to measure how well they meet your standards. You define the standards by which your employees measure their work, and you enforce discipline when things go wrong. Some employers go about this by intimidating their employees. Others "empower" their employees—too often by giving their employees tasks to accomplish but no tools with which to do so. Employees respond positively when they know what their managers want and how they can contribute. They succeed when their managers enable them to do so.

➡ **Lead by example**

You send messages to your employees every day. You tell them what's important to you by the attention you pay to this or that detail, by the questions you ask and by the reports you request. They read a lot into what you do, especially if you rarely ask for reports and then suddenly send them into a flurry of activity to get you the data you request. Get employees into the habit of consistently preparing daily, weekly and monthly reports. Insist that they start each report with an analysis of what they see there, so that the data becomes more meaningful to them over time as they are asked to interpret it. Then conduct regular group meetings to hear opposing points of view—both on the interpretation of the data and how to solve problems that are spotted by reviewing the data.

By stressing the ratios and measures you value—indeed, by showing a keen interest in these numbers—you focus your staff on the important things.

➡ **Look to the long term—the very long term.**

You won't be around forever, so plan ahead.

This is sometimes hard to appreciate, especially if you founded your own company. But it's important. Working to ensure that your company survives you helps you and your employees focus on matters of importance.

Many companies run and even thrive on personality alone—on the charismatic leader whose employees rally round for direction and inspiration.

Business Plans to Game Plans

Businesses like this can start to look more like cults than companies, though, and cult-companies often don't outlive their leaders. Companies thrive when they operate according to principles their employees can believe in. Your employees will do better if they believe that your company exists to do something more than make you wealthy. They want to know that their efforts will pay off whether you're around or not.

This does not take away from you—the person running the company—so much as it gives to your employees. You improve your own prospects for a payoff from your employees if you improve their prospects for a payoff from your company. If you show them that you expect your company to run whether you're there or not, you show that you really do look to the long term. If they do better, you do better.

➡ **Find the important details and focus on them.**

You must know all the details of your business and you must know which are critical. You must study your operations and then extract those details that are key to your success. It's not enough to house volumes of reports on a bookshelf. You must know what those reports mean. If, for example, you send out 50,000 pieces of direct mail and sales jump two weeks later, you may conclude that you dropped an effective mailing. But maybe your advertising kicked in at the same time or a distributor launched an incentive program. You must find out and acknowledge what works and what doesn't work.

And remember that data is about quantity, not quality. It measures performance by answering objective questions: How well do our results match up against our expectations? What's different? Is the trend up or down? Will these trends last a short time, or do they look long term? What might have contributed to what we see in the data? What's missing from this data that would lead us to ask more questions?

Data doesn't answer questions of quality: Is what we see good or bad? How important is what we see? How should we respond?

As a rule, the finance department is the one corporate unit devoted to quantitative analysis. It doesn't develop, produce, market or deliver the product; rather, it measures the *results* of your efforts to do all those things. It provides you with the data from which you draw the benchmarks for measuring your company's performance. This doesn't make the financial department more important than the others—simply more useful in this context.

➡ **Face reality when you look at your company data.**

The problems you encounter in running your company are tough enough to solve. Don't let confusion muddy the waters.

This means keeping your analyses as objective as possible. Admit what you see to those around you. Don't try to persuade yourself or others to see what isn't there.

You may be the only person, for example, who can tell whether a two-month downturn in revenues reflects your ordinary business cycle or the beginning of a more drastic trend. You must gauge the truth and act accordingly.

➡ **Variance may mean trouble, so keep an eye on it.**

Your business may outperform your projections. It may fall short. Either way, you need to know. A game plan allows you to monitor performance in detail, so learn how performance varies from the vision of your business plan. There are no shortcuts in preparing the information, in studying it and in acting on it. You must plan, act, measure and plan again. Don't expect to do this quickly. Analyzing the data takes time—at least twice as long as it takes to compile the data.

You may be jubilant when you outperform expectations, but just as many problems stem from too much business as too little. Are you prepared with staff and resources to accept faster growth than you initially projected? Will customers face inventory shortages or longer waits on your customer service phone lines? Take each variance as an opportunity to rethink each aspect of your business. Recognize how changes in growth will affect your business.

The Bottom Line

In this book I will show you how to turn a good business plan into an effective game plan. I want to persuade you of the importance of planning, acting, measuring, adjusting and planning again—and provide you with ways to do these things. I ask lots of questions, some tough, and call for straightforward and useful answers.

Above all, I want this book to be useful. I present tools to allow you to look inside the important areas of your company and assess where you are and what you must do to move forward. Some worksheets are diagnostic tests for existing operations; some give you an outline for future action. Collectively, they provide a disciplined system that keeps you moving ahead without reinventing the wheel.

I also want to argue the importance of every employee in this effort. I believed so strongly in the potential of every individual who worked for my company, that one of my goals as leader was to teach everyone how to run a company. I looked at each employee as a potential successor, and sought to mentor that person as I would a son or daughter who might one day run a business. I don't hold back information; on the contrary, I seek to share whatever wisdom I have gained.

Chapter 2:

Effective Business Planning

We begin both our business plan and game plan by considering our company's vision statement and mission statement. While closely related, vision and mission statements are different things.

The *vision* statement expresses what the company wants to be in the business world, whereas the *mission* statement expresses what the company does to achieve its vision. The vision statement expresses the end; the mission statement, the means. The vision statement sets the goal; the mission statement tells your employees what your company will do in order to reach that goal.

Giving Meaning to Work

When Sherry Sheng came from the Seattle Aquarium to take over as executive director of the Portland (Oregon) Zoo, she found a public entity that had lost a practical sense of the market it served. To revitalize the staff, she led all 100 employees through a rigorous self-evaluation aimed at giving meaning to their work.

Sheng used techniques more often found in the private sector than the public, looking beyond day-to-day operational concerns and creating a vision by which future decisions could be based. "You can call it strategic planning," Sheng told a local newspaper. "But it wasn't just to create some document. We needed to be able to draw out the passion of a place like this. People come to look at the animals because they get to you at a gut level."

She felt the same visceral passion could motivate employees. To capture this, she developed a vision statement for the Zoo. She worked with a variety of managers and employees—enforcing only one strict rule: the vision statement could be no longer than eight words. The statement simply reads:

Caring now for the future of life.

To Sheng, using a vision statement was merely a common sense approach. "Why does the zoo exist? We're here because we care about the future of life, about sustainability," she says. "It points to the programs we are involved in; it points to how we craft exhibits and our education programs. It also points to customer service."

Sheng and her managers have been able to develop a number of mission statements for different operations that use the vision statement as a starting point. The result: a better focused, more effective organization armed to cope with change.

By identifying where you see yourself tomorrow, you create a well-focused picture of where you stand today.

Establishing a values system that helps bring meaning to the workplace has become fairly commonplace in the private sector. So, too, has the idea of giving employees more responsibility such that they can help improve an organization's performance. But public-sector managers usually rely on more traditional, hierarchical, techniques.

Whether public sector or private, what holds true for a CEO holds true for other managers, too. In order to perform your job well, you have to start with three broad goals:

1. To create vision and mission statements that define your purpose;

2. To communicate these statements clearly and effectively; and

3. To measure and encourage progress.

If you accomplish these three goals, you've gone a long way toward realizing a fourth: to build a culture that makes your company a good place to work—and thus, improves your prospects for success. You need to give your company a strong sense of purpose.

Achieve all of this and you'll take control of your dreams. You'll be living your vision.

Practical Matters

Many owners and managers feel that a mission statement is the best tool for getting everyone in the company going in the same direction. Equally as important, developing a new or revised mission statement forces managers to think tactically.

The main goal: to avoid getting so busy managing today's business that tomorrow's gets pushed aside. Goals are most useful when they help you decide what you and other employees should be doing at work today to help you achieve what you want for the future.

This forward-looking perspective is complicated by the fact that only after a company has done some business can an owner or manager make a useful assessment about work challenges and how a company should respond. It's only after people have purchased your product that you'll find out who your market really is—rather than who you thought it would be.

Maintaining Focus

When Richard Haworth succeeded his father as president of Michigan-based Haworth, Inc. in 1976, one of the first things he did was create a mission statement, called "The Haworth Creed," summarizing the company's standards and goals.

At the time, the privately-owned manufacturer of office furniture had 250 employees and $14 million in annual sales. In 1998 it celebrated 50 years in business. And in 1999, the company had 11,000 employees worldwide and annual sales surpassing $1.5 billion.

Business Plans to Game Plans

In 1996, Haworth introduced a revised statement called "Our Principles," modernizing and simplifying the language to be more readily understood around the globe.

The Principles included a vision statement that clearly articulated the company's long-term goals. It's a simple, 21-word announcement:

Our vision is to be world class in the eyes of our customers at creating well-designed, effective and exciting work environments.

Haworth's mission statement involves more explanation. As do most effective mission statements, it describes the most likely means by which the company can realize its vision:

To completely satisfy our customers is our primary mission. We listen to our customers and understand their changing needs. We achieve their satisfaction by quickly translating these needs into products and services that are world class and that emphasize quality, design, innovation and value. We know that our success is built on satisfied customers. We believe that our customers are best served through a strong dealer network. Haworth dealers aggressively represent us and offer a range of complementary professional services to our customers. Our dealers collaborate with us to forge customer-satisfying teams. Our dealers are also our customers, and we are committed to their satisfaction.

Haworth members are the most important resource of our company and we depend on the talents of all Haworth members. Because we value differences and trust people, we try to create work environments that encourage the contributions of every member. Our members endorse the practice of continuous improvement, believing it offers the best path to pride in their work, greater job security, customer satisfaction and success for our company. Our corporate culture offers a participative environment that supports teams and individuals. Haworth encourages member development and achievement through recognition, rewards and opportunities for career growth.

In order to achieve total customer satisfaction, Haworth methods of operation are shaped by our dedication to quality. Corporate-wide quality initiatives result in superior products and services for our customers. At Haworth, we combine intelligence with hard work to eliminate wasted time, effort and materials. Our philosophy of continuous improvement is embraced by suppliers and dealers. They share our commitment to total customer satisfaction. With them, we create a seamless flow of high-quality products and services to the end user. Our philosophy includes the preservation of our environment and the protection of resources. Our pursuit of quality extends to our communities, where we build for the future by investing in the quality of life.

For Haworth, the results have been positive. It doubled sales over the past five years, was the first U.S. office furniture manufacturer to be ISO-9001 registered[1] and has been one of the best 100 companies to work for in America according to the best-selling book by that title. It intends to stay focused on its existing products and markets during the next decade.

Provide a Living Example

The best way to lead is to take your vision and mission statements seriously yourself. If you provide a living example, other people will follow. You must concentrate on the issues of employee motivation and the vision statement. If you have a clear vision statement and a motivated work force, the numbers will go a long way toward taking care of themselves.

"Most people are too close to their own situation to look objectively at what they ought to be going for. A small business operator can have a great idea, but cannot see the land mines ahead," warns Jim Morehouse, with Chicago-based consulting firm A.T. Kearny. "A wonderful entrepreneur can have great vision, but be blinded by the obstacles. Good mission and vision statements will keep them focused."

"You must get your viewpoint across clearly and concisely," says Donald

---

[1]ISO 9001 is the internationally-adopted quality assurance standard that applies to the design, development and manufacturing of products and services.

Kuratko, the Stoops Professor of Business at Ball State University. "If the vision statement is clear and concise, then it will be easier to convey to buyers, employees and the rest. Get out. Do the footwork. Touch the marketplace." It is hard to expect your employees to be focused on what your vision and mission statements say is important unless you yourself are focused."

A Glance at SWOT Analysis

To begin to make certain that the vision and mission are attainable, many companies participate in an exercise called a SWOT Analysis. SWOT stands for Strengths, Weaknesses, Opportunities and Threats. The system emphasizes a more complete perspective on what accounts for success in a company. It was originally developed by the Massachusetts-based Boston Consulting Group in the early 1970s.

SWOT Analysis is a graphic thing. It clearly maps out particular—and sometimes recurring—aspects of a company in a consistent manner. It makes disparate steps and activities easy to compare. For this reason alone, many managers use SWOT on at least an occasional basis.

Advocates say that SWOT Analysis works well because it contrasts the internal and external factors that affect a company. They argue that it matches the strengths of the company's internal environment with opportunities in the organization's external environment in a way that makes its core competencies self-evident.

Scanning the internal environment includes an analysis of the company's structure, culture and resources. Here are just some of the areas that should be considered in SWOT Analysis:

- Product quality
- Ownership structure
- Quality of the management staff
- Brand name

- Clear vision and objectives
- Quality of staff appraisal system
- Profitability
- Availability of cash for growth
- Quality of marketing and sales efforts
- Staff morale

Scanning the external environment will determine your future opportunities, but also force a company to face problems that could threaten its survival if not taken into account. Such factors include:

- Market limitations
- Lack of capital
- Problems with suppliers
- Declining market share
- Location/facility challenges
- Quality of labor pool
- Revolutionary changes in the industry

Once you've identified strengths, weaknesses, opportunities and threats, you can compare each to your vision and mission statements. Do your strengths and opportunities match your goals? Do your weaknesses and threats make your vision and mission unrealistic? If there are illogical connections or inconsistencies, what do they mean?

Setting Goals to Measure Progress

Once you have set your vision and mission, you endeavor to set performance goals by determining key success factors, corporate objectives and departmental or—ultimately—individual action plans. Specific goals for performance can accomplish several things. The most important among these: monitoring on a regular basis the progress your company makes. Simply said, goals for performance serve as yardsticks allowing you to measure how well you do the things that win business. But—like so much else that relates to managing coworkers, customers, vendors and other constituencies—their implementation isn't quite so simple.

Some experts say that a good business plan defines performance goals by itself. That's not always true. It may not even relate exactly to the quality/value/service triad of market forces. Your performance goals have more to do with the art of good management than the science of accurate financial projection.

Another way to think of performance goals: they're the practical expansion of your company's core competency. Defining them helps you extend what you do well now into what you need to do to meet your goals. Practicality is the essential aspect of setting goals for company and individual performance. Realistic goals distinguish a workable business plan from an unworkable one.

A Glance at Key Success Factors

In any monitoring process there are hundreds of measurable parameters. You need to define and track the business factors that are most important to the customer and most essential to extending your core competency.

A company's key success factors are those things that, if done well, will help assure a company that it will fulfill its mission and vision. They help bring the vision and mission into sharper focus, making clearer what series of steps must be accomplished over an indefinite period of time in order to turn vision into reality.

In most cases, it helps to consider every process as a series of set check points or benchmarks. What specific things do you have to do well to accomplish a specific end? To develop a new product? To make that product? To sell it? To ship it?

When you've determined the necessary activities that go into each step in your business process, take a moment and ask three important questions: Do your customers value these activities? How do you use your assets to accomplish these success factors? And how do you measure performance?

For many manufacturers, the ratio of orders to cash is a key success factor. This tells them how likely they are to meet a specific order in a given amount of time. Other companies use projected revenue-per-employee ratios or inventory turnover as key factors. Beginning in the late 1980s, American car makers put a lot of emphasis on new product development that met the needs of an economy-conscious public. That's a key success factor, too.

Most managers find it easiest to break out key success factors along the primary business functions we've discussed before—finance, marketing and product development, sales and customer service, operations and human resources.

Finance

In many ways, you'll have the easiest time determining key success factors and setting up performance goals for your finance department. Finance is all about measurement. It's always good to stress clarity, because financial people will sometimes mistake intricacy for completeness.

Focus on the traditional performance parameters that most companies have to meet—unit cost, return on investment, cash flow and profit margin. The challenge in setting financial objectives often has less to do with numbers you target than with translating those numbers to your coworkers. You want everyone in your company to understand cost-basis and cash flow, to say—or at least think: "I sold X plus 20 percent. My costs were Y minus three percent. My cash flow is greater than I thought it would be."

Sometimes it's necessary to refine your financial perspective, adjust a product line, eliminate low-volume or low-margin products or restructure operations. All of these activities are the appropriate results of particular goals that your finance people have to meet.

The regular revision of financial objectives sets up a level of discipline. You should monitor financial performance constantly. Monthly is essential—weekly is better. For many, data is now available in real time, but don't confuse the availability of data with the analysis of the data. Analysis should still be done at least monthly, but probably not daily.

Marketing and Product Development

Marketing is about information. Marketing performance standards should give you useful information about your industry sector, your competition, services you need to provide, relevant customer demographics and anything else that relates to what you make and how you make it.

In marketing circles, experts talk about the six P's: product, price, packaging, purchasing trends, public response and profitability. You should make sure that your standards include the tracking of practical information.

Some managers (especially at smaller companies) make the mistake of thinking of marketing as a process that stops when the actual selling of a product begins. While your marketing department may play a bigger role in the early part of a product's life cycle, it should provide you with information throughout. Your marketing department should serve as an early-warning system for changes in your business.

Putting It in Writing

Developing a consistent strategy based on key success factors in marketing and in finance helped turn around North Carolina-based Healthtex, Inc., a children's clothing company that had gone through some significant ownership changes during the 1970s and 1980s. Starting in the early 1990s, Healthtex president and CEO Gary Simmons and his management team decided they needed to put in writing what Healthtex wanted to do and who its target customers were.

The vision statement devised by Healthtex is so short that management printed it on plastic cards that employees could easily carry in their wallets. The statement reads:

Chapter 2: Effective Business Planning

Healthtex will be the most responsive kidswear company in understanding and meeting the needs of targeted consumers and retailers with basic and fashion-everyday playwear that lasts.

The company identified its primary customer as a mother of newborn to six-year-old children, who shops for everyday playwear in middle-market department stores and national children's specialty chains.

"We now are a profitable company and are now moving forward very nicely," Simmons says. "The goal here is that everybody—be it a machine operator, a designer or the head of human resources—is thinking in a similar vein. It doesn't mean they all think alike, but at least they all have a central core belief of what this company's trying to achieve." Thus, the statement has helped by getting different groups of people within the company to focus on a strategic direction.

Simmons says he tries to limit the number of goals he sets for the company at any given time. "Fifteen goals take people away from the major mission," he says. "We have three to five instead—all team-based goals we try to accomplish on a yearly basis."

In addition, Healthtex has key success factors based in six financial areas that it calls "gold standards." These include:

- Profit margin
- Operating profit
- Sales and general administrative costs
- Cost of capital
- Bottom line profit
- Return on assets

Simmons and his senior managers set specific numbers as targets for each ratio every year. "If you achieve all of these, you've done well," he says.

And Healthtex has. The company experienced high revenue growth during the mid-1990s—40 percent growth over two consecutive years. Although sales have plateaued for the past two years, profits continue to increase. Healthtex has also launched into e-commerce with a Web site geared toward its retail outlets. Since retailers can now buy on-line instead of the traditional method of purchasing at trade shows, Healthtex ultimately intends to pursue Web sales to consumers, offering their customers a full line of products. Most retailers typically offer only a few of their hundreds of products at each individual store; Web retailing opens new doors for profit.

Sales and Customer Service

Your sales performance, like your financial performance, is easy to track. But sales performance goals must be tied to profitability goals or you may win the battle and lose the war. We generally measure a company's growth in terms of its revenues, but a revenue reduction with a profit increase is the beginning of a legitimate strategy for growth.

Operations

The purpose of performance goals for operations is to get higher-quality products to market faster and at a lower cost than your competitors. And you should think of your own historical performance as a competitor.

Basically, you need to determine what levels of capacity, capability and performance (and what—if any—changes in policy, procedures and practices) you need from operations to reach company-wide goals. Some specific examples:

- How much equipment, process capacity and facility space is needed?

- Where should this design, equipment, process capacity and facility space be located?

- What kinds of design, management information and control, materials and resources and distribution systems are needed to support your projections?

- Do your operating policies, procedures and practices support the plan?

Operations performance goals act as a kind of fail-safe test of broader goals. If the cost of providing or correcting these resources exceeds the practical limits set up in your budget, you'll have to prioritize your company-wide goals and make decisions about which goals you can realistically meet. Or, on the other hand, where you're willing to exceed your limits in order to meet your goals.

Human Resources

Human resource goals exist to help provide the structure and motivation in making the other performance goals possible. Individuals working together toward a shared goal are unstoppable. But the distractions caused by people not working in concert and, in some cases, intentionally thwarting the progress, make all other goals impossible to attain.

Human resource performance goals center on having a focused and motivated group working and communicating well together to achieve the vision of the company. A company must take a hard look at its culture, probably with outside assessment tools, in order to see what is keeping it from having that focused team. Sometimes it is a lack of clear policies or a lack of enforcement. Sometimes the compensation structure is not reasonable. More often, however, it is the lack of communication.

Another part of human resource goals is ensuring that you have the most appropriate or qualified team members. To this end, ask the following questions: What is the company's turnover rate? Are you losing valuable employees to competitors? Do employees receive regular feedback on their performance and the performance of their department? Is compensation tied to the kind of performance you want? Are employees receiving regular training in job skills and in communications skills? Are you experiencing increasing absenteeism? Are employees having to work more overtime than is reasonable? Have employees been injured on the job? It is just as important to set goals in these areas as in all of the others.

An Explicit Connection

Maine-based Lepage Bakeries is one of New England's biggest commercial baking operations. The company uses its vision statement as part of an integrated system of continuing improvement and quality goals.

"We weren't a company attempting to right an ill by bringing in a new system of communication management," says chairman Albert Lepage. "We discovered that many of the things we were doing already were MTQ."

MTQ—an acronym for "Managing Total Quality"—influences much of the company's operations. It helped develop a vision statement, which the bakery's executive management group hammered out during a company retreat in the fall of 1992. The statement articulates in plain language where the managers wanted the company to be:

> *The Lepage Bakeries' vision is to be the most consistent, productive and respected baking company, to exceed customer expectations and to provide an ever-increasing economic opportunity for all of those associated with Lepage Bakeries.*

Once this vision had been defined, Lepage Bakeries had to get to the difficult business of communicating it to employees spread throughout Maine and New Hampshire. They began by using the vision as the basis for a strategic quality statement:

> *Our quality policy states that everyone who works with Lepage Bakeries will be honest, sincere, willing to learn, cooperate, communicate and work as a team to help Lepage Bakeries achieve its vision.*

This quality statement simply made explicit the connection between the vision and each employee's role in its implementation. It became the company's main tool for communicating its vision.

Next, the bakery's executives created a list of projects on which teams of employees from a cross-section of the company could work to implement the vision. From this list, the executives selected what they thought were the three most critical projects to attack within the first year of the quality-management process. The first projects were:

- Formalizing consistent performance evaluations throughout all facilities;
- Reducing defective products; and
- Developing at least one new product using existing facilities and equipment.

Albert Lepage says the projects serve a variety of purposes simultaneously. They streamline troublesome functions, bring together people from disparate ends of the company and—most importantly—give employees comprehensible objectives through which to understand the company's vision.

Over the past five years, the company has used this method to accomplish a variety of growth-oriented projects. Most recently, the company's investments have focused on technology, using robotics and automation to reduce costs while keeping quality high.

Corporate Objectives and Action Plans: An Overview

Listing your corporate objectives narrows things even further. Here you answer the question: What do we have to do—and when—to capitalize on our key success factors? If, for example, you consider high customer-responsiveness a key success factor, you might conclude that your marketing department needs to survey your customers on this subject a couple times a year. If you consider finding and retaining high value customers a key success factor, you might direct your accounting and sales departments to analyze your best current customers and how you sell to them.

Setting corporate objectives is generally done on an annual basis, so that work you decide to do is the next step toward your vision—work that can and should be done right away, in the next 12 months. This is where we begin to put a timetable to the planning work that has come before.

Once you decide what to do, you have to decide who does the work—and this takes you to the action plan. Here you break down the workload by department, team and individual. You let each one know what part he plays in the overall plan, when he must complete a given task and how he can measure his own success.

Participative Planning

The management process you use to develop and implement a business plan will affect the quality of the results you achieve. In the traditional mode of planning, a central group formulates strategy for management that is later issued to line personnel. This method of planning and implementation originates in a vacuum and communicates through inefficient channels. All too often, it leads to misunderstandings, frustrations and a lack of support from the personnel who are expected to carry out the strategy. They feel no responsibility or sense of ownership for the plan or results since they had no involvement in the planning process. In the modern economy, no company can afford this level of detachment.

The best alternative is a more participative approach. This involves creating cross-functional teams of empowered line management and staff specialists in the development of functional strategies. The specialists may be employees, consultants or a combination of both. Such participative approaches are more likely to generate the understanding, patience and support you need to implement your business plan successfully.

While the vision, mission, SWOT and key success factors may be determined primarily by a management team, this is where the process shifts to be driven bottom-up. The results of the planning work to this point should be shared with the rest of the employees and their response should drive the remainder of the process. Often the corporate objectives, and department and individual action plans will be more aggressive if determined by the employees than if they were determined by management. Giving employees the opportunity to set their own goals frees both their creativity and their spirit.

Paul Giddens, manager of human resources planning for Ohio-based General Electric Aircraft Engines, says business and industry have to nurture "the environment where people can contribute to the limits of their abilities and get the motivation to improve their competence."

Giddens says that owners and managers have to start thinking like the Wizard of Oz. In that story, Giddens reminds managers, "the wizard, who is a phony, gives the scarecrow a diploma [and says] 'Now go act like you're smart.' He has been smart all along."

Likewise, a manager can't actually empower workers. But that manager can persuade them to use the power within themselves. Some management consultants refer to this kind of exceptional effort as a "defining moment." They'll tell you that defining moments are contagious. When one employee exhibits exceptional commitment, others will follow. Your mission statement tells them where to channel that commitment.

When a coworker makes an exceptional effort to do something right or fix something that's wrong, you have a good indicator that your mission statement works.

A 1991 survey of line managers taken by *Industry Week* magazine and the Wyatt Co., an Illinois-based management consulting firm, supported the practicality of employee empowerment. Of the respondents from companies with explicit programs dedicated to employee involvement in management decisions, 76 percent reported improved quality, 73 percent increased productivity and 59 percent increased profitability.

A Direct Stake

In the early 1990s, Emery Worldwide Inc. was losing nearly a million dollars a day. The company had not turned a profit since 1985. Its problem: It had strayed away from its original focus and tried to become a full-service shipping company. Within a few years, with refined and clearly-communicated performance standards, the airfreight carrier turned its past performance around.

Business Plans to Game Plans

Emery president and CEO Roger Curry said four steps led Emery to profitability. The first was communicating its business plan's marketing and operations goals to employees and the marketplace in general.

Curry stressed the importance of the company's mission statement by repeating it like a company mantra:

> *We are an airfreight company...providing time-definite transportation services to handle our customers' parcel, package and freight shipments five pounds and up around the world.*

Part of articulating that mission statement was proving to Emery staff that management would stick with it to provide a foundation for the corporate culture. The company had lost its focus through several ownership and management changes.

The second step stemmed from the first. Once it communicated the mission statement, Emery had to get down to the business of reshaping itself. It had to take a hard look at its strengths and weaknesses and build on its strengths. "We had to reconfigure operations to improve our service and efficiency, with vigilance on cost control," Curry says. "As part of that plan, we de-emphasized the envelope business, in which we had only a modest market share at best."

Many of the company's best customers operate globally and look for one company to manage all elements of the supply chain. To satisfy them, Emery introduced Logistics Worldwide, an international multi-modal logistics and information service. The airfreight carrier's foundation for such a service was already in place.

The next step was to get employees excited and give them the confidence they needed to "Make Emery a Great Company," as the company's internal publicity exhorted. Marketing plans and strategic goals were communicated throughout the company, with simplified projections posted in central facilities. Management spent six months concentrating on making the new focus known to everyone from mid-level managers to entry-level freight handlers.

The final step was to give employees a direct stake in the business improvements. Non-union employees received an incentive compensation plan to share in the airfreight carrier's profits from 1993.

The strategy worked. Today, Emery is among the leaders in market share for packages over 70 pounds. It also boasts a 99 percent on-time record, one of the best in the business. Emery's international operations currently generate about one-third of the company's total revenues. It provides service in 229 countires, with 1,300 employees and more than 560 service centers divided among four international sectors.

The Bottom Line

When you've set the basic objectives you need to run a company efficiently, you'll usually find that you've done a lot more work than you initially realized.

These tools don't always come easily to entrepreneurial managers. You might doubt the value of something as abstract as a vision statement. But give the matter a chance—exercises that seem simplistic to you may have a fundamental impact on your employees or customers.

You need to think of your business as a process in which every person involved plays an indispensable role—or they don't exist. And this process is ongoing, as long as your company is in business. It's not over when your salespeople sign a customer. It's not over when you cash that customer's check. It's not over when you ship your product.

If ever, it's over when the phone rings again and the same customer places another order. And then the whole process starts once more.

When you've finished working through the exercises in this chapter, you should have a good idea of the best practical goals you can set for your company. You should be able to look toward the horizon without tripping over any obstacles at your feet.

These pages elaborate on what we've already touched upon, with worksheets included to help you assess your business. Use them to reflect honestly on the nature and state of your company.

Vision Statement

Vision is what a leader gives his or her followers. It is his challenge to himself and to the world. It's the match that lights the fire of potential in people. It keeps a company on track in good times and bad.

To have and communicate a vision defines leadership. This is the statement of your decision to act, and a definition for what direction that action will take. You cannot lead a group of people unless you set a direction.

A vision statement uses the future to help analyze the present. As the head of your operation, you have to articulate the blend of present and future. Expressing corporate purpose is a crucial task for management.

A company needs a vision statement that everyone from the CEO to the receptionist can understand. It formulates what an organization wants to be and stimulates specific goals that can be passed down to every department in the organization. It needs to be something useful and applicable to daily operations. You—and, more importantly, your co-workers—should feel comfortable using your vision statement in everyday conversation.

What does your company do? Why does it do it? In a world where advances in automation and productivity have transformed many traditional value-added businesses into commodities, successful companies need a strong sense of purpose.

Although you are excited about your new vision, you see it clearly and you're motivated to change your organization, you still have to make certain your coworkers feel the same way that you do.

What's in a Vision

Vision means something to people at all levels in an organization. Lower-level employees might not know the specifics of the company's marketing plans or financial outlook, but they do know its reputation. They know how other players in the industry or local markets perceive it. They know when they work for a quality-driven organization, or one that's content to skim margins from second- or third-rate work.

If you build an environment that values quality, in which people can be proud of their efforts, you'll find better people more easily. And you'll be able to keep them once you've found them. But you can't achieve quality without explicitly saying you want to achieve it. It isn't something people infer from all companies. It isn't something you can receive passively. You have to set it up as a goal and continuously pursue it.

Something you'll find as you do this: people—employees, vendors and customers—want to believe in quality. Quality is rare enough that it has intrinsic value. People will work hard when they understand a vision that seeks quality performance. That kind of vision empowers people to perform well.

Results come when people develop a shared vision of how they want their organization to be perceived and are willing to work every day to maintain that vision.

Sam Walton had a vision for Wal-Mart. He believed that giving median to low-end retail customers in smaller geographic markets the widest possible choice of inexpensive goods would establish his chain as the market leader among discount department stores. His vision was this:

> *To offer all the fine customers in our territories all of their household needs in a manner in which they continue to think of us fondly.*

For McDonald's, Ray Kroc believed that cleanliness and consistency were the key ingredients to the success of his restaurants. The goal of the McDonald's chain is that the food in all of its stores—all over the world— tastes exactly the same. And that all the bathrooms are reasonably clean. This is clearly stated in the McDonald's vision:

> *To offer the fast food customer food prepared in the same high-quality manner worldwide, tasty and reasonably priced, delivered in a consistent low-key décor and friendly atmosphere.*

Business Plans to Game Plans

What is remarkable is that so many employees at all levels in both these organizations still share the founder's original vision.

First, spend time talking with someone close to you about your company and your dreams for it. Why you started it, what you wanted to accomplish, what you want to leave behind.

A vision statement is not easy to write in a sentence or two, but writing it will make it clear to you and meaningful to others.

It must have several elements: it must be long-term, meaningful in a human context and appeal to a higher purpose.

What do good vision statements have in common? You feel you know the company when you read them. They give the company a human feeling—a personality. They set out what the company values. They often refer to quality of life issues.

Try several drafts of your vision on the following page. Answer the questions. Ask people, particularly your employees, to look at your answers.

Ask Yourself:

☐ Does your vision statement answer these questions:

Who are you as a company?

Where do you want to make your mark?

How high do you want to shoot?

What do you believe in?

☐ Does what you have written embody the spirit of where you want your company to head?

☐ Can you live with this vision? Are you willing to (or more appropriately, do you automatically) act in accordance with your vision?

Vision Statement

What do you see your company becoming in five to 10 years?

_____

_____

_____

What are your values?

_____

_____

_____

_____

What will your customers be looking for?

_____

_____

_____

Draft of your vision statement:

_____

_____

_____

_____

Mission Statement

What the vision statement is to strategy, the mission statement is to tactics. It identifies the critical processes that impact implementation of vision. The vision statement will endure much longer than the mission statement. The vision statement will only change if the core purpose of the business changes. Conversely, the mission statement may change as competition or technology changes.

A good mission statement gets people to act in agreement with the company's broader goals. It reminds them how to behave every day, regardless of what temporary forces work against them, so that they can help realize the company's vision.

You should have at least one mission statement for your company—and you may develop related ones for each distinct department or division. You may also want to develop temporary mission statements to communicate a current focus.

The mission of a company is not dreamy, like a vision. It is based in today and reality. It defines specifically your product and your market—who you will sell to and what you will sell. Industrial psychologists and management consultants as diverse as Wikham Skinner and Tom Peters argue that the mission statement represents a crucial conceptual link between the business or corporate strategy and the operating functions.

A complete mission statement clearly and fully describes what factors—and, if necessary, what resources—are most critical to supporting the business strategy. The three factors that most managers consider in terms of their mission: quality, value and service.

Quality and reliability must be defined in terms of the customer and projected back to determine their impact on engineering and manufacturing. Internal quality benchmarks, as useful as they can be in monitoring operations, don't play so vital a role in developing a mission statement. You have to consider the level and meaning of quality and reliability appropriate to the desired competitive position in the marketplace.

Value can mean lowest manufacturing cost, lowest selling price or best value when other factors are considered. The first two definitions are fairly straight forward. Even though many management gurus stress so-called "best value," that definition tends to be so vague that it's useless.

Service includes more than just the friendliness of the greeting a customer hears when your receptionist picks up the phone. It translates into the degree to which you can devote company resources to the needs of a specific customer—without ignoring all others. As we'll consider later on, this has a lot to do with operations. Service entails manufacturing flexibility and versatility, the ability to produce a large variety of products of various volumes to supply a diverse market. And to do so quickly.

Particular companies consider hundreds of other factors, though in some manner almost all trace back to these basic three.

No organization can succeed by concentrating on any one of these factors to the exclusion of the other two. Your challenge is to balance the resources you apply to each in proportion to priorities based on current situations and future positions.

Management should agree on functional mission statements that identify the operating resources that are critical to support the business strategy. For example, Dominos Pizza made a dramatic change in emphasis when it changed its mission statement. Dominos was known in the pizza delivery business for its 30 minute delivery guarantee. It discontinued its 30 minute guarantee in 1993 and replaced it with this simple statement: "Made fresh, arrives fresh." In those few words, the company shifted its corporate emphasis from speed to quality. And it paid off.

While a mission statement can be as simple as defining the product and the market, some companies feel that the way they treat employees and customers is equally as important in defining who they are.

Since the late 1980s, the big players in the U.S. automobile industry have focused mission statements on reducing new product realization (the time passing from concept to the cars in the showroom) from 48 months to the 12 months that carmakers like Honda can boast. Ford, GM and Chrysler have all raised their quality standards to match their foreign competitors,

Mission Statement

What do you sell?

_____

_____

To whom do you sell?

_____

_____

What does your company do better or want to do better than anyone else?

_____

_____

How does your company rank the importance of quality, value and service?

_____

_____

How do you define each of these based on customer needs and expectations?

_____

_____

How will you achieve your vision?

_____

_____

Draft of your mission statement:

_____

_____

_____

but they suffer in comparison because they take so long to respond to market demands.

How you define your product will greatly influence how you approach product development and marketing. If you think you sell cars, then you might not think of yourself as the provider of a moving environment. You might think your customers are simply coming to buy a car. But what would they ask for if a car did not exist? They would want something that could comfortably, safely and reasonably inexpensively move them from one place to another—anywhere, even difficult to reach locations. Defining your product by solving customer problems is essential.

Define What You Do

How you define what you do should be clearly tied in with your company's core competency. Your core competency is the thing that you do best. It is the strongest of your strengths. In my company's case, it was taking complex data and translating it into something simple to understand and simple to use. The Nordstrom department store's core competency is in developing a relationship with customers. Accordingly, it defines its product as the service its sales associates add to the value of merchandise with this statement:

Exceptional service, selection, quality and value.

The discussion that can lead to preparing this portion of the mission statement may be the most important part of creating it. To be able to clearly define your market may be a more difficult task than you would think.

Look at your own promotional catalogs to see if all of your products have a similar theme that you can define. Like Federal Express, is your primary product speed? Like Nordstrom, is your primary product quality in terms of service? Or like Apple computer, is your primary product quality in terms of ease of installation and use? Like Wal-Mart, is your primary product wide selection?

Get a list of your customers and look for their similarities. Is your market who you thought they would be? Can everyone who buys from you be classified as a particular group? Or like Fed Ex, is your market almost everyone?

Take these preliminary ideas to your employees and see if they agree. Have meetings just to discuss these items. Then test them in the outside world. Circulate your drafts; edit and rewrite them until you feel good about them.

Ask Yourself:

☐ Does your mission statement capture what makes you unique as a company?

☐ Would your customers and vendors recognize you in these statements? Would they be pleasantly surprised because they could really buy in to these directions?

☐ Would your customers agree with your directions?

☐ Is your mission statement inspiring?

☐ Does this give everyone in your company a direction for each day when they walk in the door? Is there any ambiguity in what is most important?

☐ If an employee faced a difficult dilemma at work, would thinking of your mission statement lead them to make the right decision?

SWOT Analysis

Competitive advantage is usually divided into two kinds: internal and external. The analysis of the internal environment and the external environment comes together in the SWOT (Strengths, Weaknesses, Opportunities and Threats) analysis. The point of this exercise is to first match the strengths found in the company's internal environment with opportunities in the organization's external environment.

Companies should employ resources in a manner consistent with the given source of competitive advantage they pursue. Before you can make a decision about reacting to an opportunity or threat, you have to understand your own strengths and weaknesses. And you have to believe that your understanding is valid.

Once a company knows where it's going, it should be able to assess where it currently stands so it can see how far it has to go. The SWOT analysis is a tool for looking internally—at your company's strengths and weaknesses—as well as externally for the opportunities and threats that come to you from outside.

This is a tool often used for a group discussion among key people and for good feedback to management on how employees view the company. A SWOT analysis can be done for the company as a whole, as well as for various departments. This is how I use it:

Strengths. Our strengths are our core competencies—those things we do better than any of our competitors or that really tie together all the products we offer in a unique way. What internal structures or expertise do we have that are a special source of pride? This becomes the center for determining what we will do in the future. We want to constantly build on the things we already do particularly well.

Weaknesses. For every thing we visualize clearly or do well, there is something we can't see so clearly or do so well. Some of these weaknesses we can change—others we can't. Where do we need to build our company? What is holding us back or creating a bottleneck for everyone else? If we choose to spend money or other resources in one direction, in what other directions might we be tolerating or creating weaknesses?

Business Plans to Game Plans

Some examples of strengths and weaknesses were mentioned earlier in the chapter. Others are listed below and can be found in each of our core areas:

- Reputation for service
- Responsiveness to market
- Business growth
- Leadership
- Product innovation
- Reporting and analysis
- Cost controls
- Employee morale
- Performance feedback
- Recruiting qualified employees
- Training
- Communications
- Compensation
- Benefits
- Physical Facility
- Information systems

Opportunities. The most difficult aspect about opportunity is recognizing it. The old adage about opportunity knocking once does apply in many cases, so we need to see it—and be able to act on it—when it comes. What are our greatest challenges in the changing environment of the industries we serve? How will new technologies help us? What will our customers need in the future that we can supply? What opportunities will open up globally?

Threats. As with weaknesses, there are some threats we can minimize and others we can't. We need to do all we can to control the threats we can predict—and prepare for the ones we can't. What outside our control could threaten our existence? How might new technology hurt us? What in the political environment (government) might threaten us? Will ups or downs in the economy hurt us? What in our physical environment might threaten us?

Make many copies of the worksheet on the following page, give them to key staff members and ask them for their analysis independently. Then ask for all the input brought in from each member of the group in each of the four categories. Write out all ideas on a board in front of the group, and then pick seven to 10 of the items in each category that seem best to fit your company. As with many management issues, the challenge for you is to judge well which items under each heading are key and which aren't.

Ask Yourself:

☐ Are you using your strengths to their fullest capacity? Are they things you could leverage by teaching them to more people in order to develop more product, market better or be more efficient?

☐ Do you celebrate what you do well?

☐ Why have you chosen to live with your weaknesses? Would eliminating these be painful? Result in difficult staff changes or cultural changes? Are they financially costly to resolve?

☐ What is holding you back from taking the most advantage of your opportunities?

☐ Are your competitors taking better advantage of these than you are?

☐ What can you do immediately to minimize threats?

☐ Do you have plans to minimize the damage if any of these threats becomes a reality?

SWOT Analysis

Date _____

Strengths	Weaknesses
Opportunities	**Threats**

Key Success Factors

The purpose here is to answer the question: What are the key things that, if we do them well, will ensure our success as a business? The answer may not be easy or obvious, but I believe it is all part of narrowing down the business plan to the vision and then to the mission. This process will eventually lead to implementation.

Key success factors are similar to vision as corporate objectives are similar to mission. Key success factors are fairly broad and do not have a time horizon, but they are an essential link between the vision and mission, and the creation of time-specific corporate objectives.

Business owners set goals and objectives. But are they the goals that will relate to business success? If you know those items that, if done, will make you successful, you can set objectives that will ensure you are on track. Setting objectives without first determining your key success factors may mean you are not setting objectives that relate to the success of your business.

As with mission and vision statements, don't identify and publish key success factors that you're not willing to validate with your own actions. If you say the highest quality products are essential, don't allow your employees to ship products they know and you know don't meet standards.

Many time management books preach that you should always be doing the most important things you have to accomplish. Don't waste precious time on small things. Do first things first. Key success factors are a critical element for deciding what is most important. Imagine that every item accomplished by an employee every day related directly to one of those items you have decided are key for success. Would productivity increase?

Fill in the blanks of the sentence: "If we _____,

_____

then we will be successful." (There are spaces in the worksheet for three key factors for each of the business functions—finance, marketing and product development, sales and customer service, operations and human resources. Add more if they relate to you.)

My company's 10 key success factors, by business function, were:

Finance

1. Sell each unit at a profit.

Selling each unit at a profit means controling costs above the gross margin line (those costs that relate directly to producing the product), including the costs of sales and marketing. Selling each unit at a profit insists that you won't continue to produce products or product lines that aren't adding to the bottom line. This doesn't necessarily mean you will discontinue a struggling new product, but you'll have to consider whether you can cut its production or selling costs to make it worth keeping.

2. Continue to reduce overhead costs.

Reducing overhead costs relates to costs in the personnel, facilities, and administrative expense section of your income statement.[2] Most companies make an effort every few years to reduce overhead, particularly when economic times are hard. But when sales are up and the profit picture is good, these expenses tend to creep up. It is important to constantly monitor overhead, and continually keep pressure on to reevaluate these costs on an ongoing basis.

Both of these items are essential to your ability to stay profitable. Even if you accomplish all of your other key success factors, but are unable to do this profitably, you won't be able to stay in business very long.

Marketing and Product Development

3. Develop new products that capture the needs of our customers, while keeping current products high quality.

It's hard to imagine not having the success of your business tied in to continually creating better products, if for no other reason than to give your marketing and sales people something new to sell. Customer expectations about product variety, in terms of products fitting their exact needs, increase every year. The ability of customers to determine where else to buy a similar product increases as well with the increase in communication technologies. You must continually do it better or be prepared to lose business.

---

[2]See pages 140-143, Year at a Glance Income Statement

4. Determine the right Internet strategy.

Many companies are spending what may (or may not) be a disproportionate amount of their resources pursuing an Internet strategy. It is important to aggressively pursue these strategies that may dramatically reduce costs, but also to be sure traditional sources of sales are not neglected in the process. It is a high-risk and high-reward time for many companies.

Sales and Customer Service

5. Find and retain high-value customers.

One of the factors critical to your success may be retaining business from your top five or six customers, who may account for the majority of your total sales. If no one in the company realizes the importance of these large accounts, managers may set primary objectives to get new business or focus on overall customer service. If you don't define and communicate the critical elements, your coworkers will not necessarily design a strategy to retain your top customers, and those crucial customers may take their business to your competition.

6. Create and maintain the highest level of customer satisfaction.

Decide who will likely buy your product, make sure they know it exists, offer them easy ways to purchase it and make sure they buy again by providing outstanding customer service. If none of your key success factors has to do with serving the customer better, you probably won't be in business very long.

At my company, I wanted customers to come away with more than they expected. Our business was built on a base that we earned over the course of time. Some of our customers had been buying from us for nearly 40 years. Can you imagine the value of a 40-year customer?

Operations

7. Continue to use technology to improve quality.

Some owners and managers overlook key success factors related to operations. That's a mistake—they are central to profitability. Operations

Key Success Factors

For the Upcoming Year We Will
Concentrate Our Efforts in These Areas

Finance	Marketing and Product Development
Key Success Factor #_____ If we . . . _____ _____ then we will be successful. Key Success Factor #_____ If we . . . _____ _____ then we will be successful. Key Success Factor #_____ If we . . . _____ _____ then we will be successful.	Key Success Factor #_____ If we . . . _____ _____ then we will be successful. Key Success Factor #_____ If we . . . _____ _____ then we will be successful. Key Success Factor #_____ If we . . . _____ _____ then we will be successful.
Sales and Customer Service	**Operations and Human Resources**
Key Success Factor #_____ If we . . . _____ _____ then we will be successful. Key Success Factor #_____ If we . . . _____ _____ then we will be successful. Key Success Factor #_____ If we . . . _____ _____ then we will be successful.	Key Success Factor #_____ If we . . . _____ _____ then we will be successful. Key Success Factor #_____ If we . . . _____ _____ then we will be successful. Key Success Factor #_____ If we . . . _____ _____ then we will be successful.

includes the whole process of getting your product to the people who want it, from prototype to customers' hands. This means how you process orders, fulfill and ship so that customers get what they want the first time and on time.

8. Get products to market quickly, effectively and accurately.

These processes should be continually improved, just like your product. If the time from prototype to market-ready product is three months, what would you have to do to reduce it to one month? If you currently ship product within five days, what would you have to do to ship within 48 hours? And, most pertinent to this discussion, what processes most impact profits and customer satisfaction? These may be your key success factors.

Do you often wonder why an employee is working on one project when it is obvious to you that the project that has been sitting in an in-box for three weeks is the more critical one? Maybe you failed to communicate affectively what is important to you. Key success factors communicate which project to do first. Since they start at the top, everyone knows that what she does relates to what the company as a whole does. Key success factors are not phrases like "we need to be profitable" or "we need to stay ahead of the competition." These words do not relate enough to the purpose of the business, nor do they lead employees in any direction.

Human Resources

9. Find and retain high-value employees.

10. Compensate employees to clearly pay for excellent performance.

In addition to setting and communicating your visions and expectations, assembling the best staff you can is an important challenge. The people you hire and how you treat them says more about your philosophy than any vision statement ever will. Employees are key to your success, and you should set objectives every year regarding better training, increasing benefits, systems of compensation, reviewing performance, etc.

Don't continually improve your products and services without continually improving your personnel and what you offer them.

As with vision and mission statements, route these forms to key employees and then compare responses to check for anything you might have missed.

Ask Yourself:

☐ Do your key success factors encompass all the important areas of your business? Do they truly represent what would make you successful?

☐ If your competitors did the same things, would they be successful?

☐ What percentage of your time (personally) and your company's time is spent on making these things happen? If it isn't most of your time, why not? What else is more important?

☐ Do your employees all know that these factors are critical? What ways do you have of telling them?

Corporate Objectives

Key success factors clarify what we think we must do to make the business succeed in a general sense. Corporate objectives turn these key success factors into specific items to be accomplished. They should also be written to include specific measurements to know if success has been achieved.

To look at how corporate objectives differ from key success factors, I have taken our key success factors and suggested a sample of one objective that relates to each of them.

Later in this chapter you will find one worksheet for each of the major business functions—finance, marketing and product development, sales and customer service, operations and human resources.

Key Success Factor #1: Sell each unit at a profit.

Objective #1-1: Reduce costs of Product A to create a 55 percent gross profit margin.

All products must pull their own weight. Traditionally, we seem to have very profitable products that are pulled down by others that do not justify themselves. One objective is to look at product modifications to reduce the expense of a given product so that its current sales will be profitable.

Key Success Factor #2: Continue to reduce overhead costs.

Objective #2-1: Reduce administrative costs to 15 percent of sales.

This is an ongoing objective for my company. The lower overhead can be, the better. Overhead items (to be discussed in great detail in the financial section) are necessary, but do not add to the making of the product or the marketing of it.

Our objectives usually include reducing reliance on outside services, looking into more effective ways of using insurance, reduction of office supply use, etc.

Key Success Factor #3: Develop new products that capture the needs of our customers, while keeping current products high quality.

Objective #3-1: Work with Customer A to develop a new product that will meet the training needs outlined in their performance goals for the year.

Objectives in this category might relate to changes in each specific product, and how many new products you intend to create. Deadlines for completion are very important to make sure designers are not continually making something better, but never getting the improved design out to customers.

Key Success Factor #4. Determine the right Internet strategy.

Objective #4-1: Produce 10 percent of our sales leads through Internet registration by potential customers.

Objectives in this category might be a goal for actual sales via the Web, number of hits for your site or improving the quality of information or the interactivity of your Web presence.

Key Success Factor #5: Find and retain high-value customers.

Objective #5-1: Add 10 new $100,000 sales volume per year customers.

Each word in this key success factor is meaningful. We seek a specific customer, but not everyone in our target market. The kind of customers we want are high value. They value what we value in our product and our service, and our relationship with them is profitable for us as well as for them. We not only want to find them, we want to do our best to retain them.

If finding and retaining high-quality customers is important, you might:

- develop methods to get feedback from customers, such as surveys;

- streamline procedures, making it easier to order and return your products; and

- consider the quality of your promotional material to determine whether it accurately describes your products.

Key Success Factor #6: Create and maintain the highest level of customer satisfaction.

Objective #6-1: Return all Web site queries within 24 hours.

With this statement we aim to create the highest level of service to our customers. And once created, do what it takes to maintain that service level. Objectives might include: setting up an ongoing customer contact program, focusing on special services for your top-10 dollar-volume customers, etc.

Key Success Factor #7: Get products to market quickly, effectively and accurately.

Objective #7-1: Set up real time Internet tracking for all orders.

It would be hard to imagine a set of corporate objectives today without extensive reference to quality enhancements through technology. Either to benefit the customer or internal operations or both, communication via the Internet for taking orders, tracking shipping, need for information or solving problems is a high priority.

Key Success Factor #8: Continue to use technology to improve quality.

Objective #8-1: Reduce inventory turn to 30 days.

Objectives will relate to time and quality standards. Time issues must usually be balanced against quality issues. The more specific these objectives can be, the better. You may wish to set goals such as all orders being shipped the same day, or adequate inventory levels to assure backorders do not occur.

Key Success Factor #9: Find and retain high-value employees.

Objective #9-1: Institute a 360 degree performance appraisal system.

Objectives here relate to hiring in new or strategically important areas, training or letting go of weaker team members, better performance feedback, etc. You may set objectives for dollar volume sales per employee, or reviewing and revising your employee policy handbook.

Key Success Factor #10: Compensate employees to clearly pay for excellent performance.

Objective #10-1: Review the current compensation system and make sure base compensation is industry competitive.

Compensation is a highly specialized area and we have frequently sought outside help to bring in the expertise and the objectivity to deal with pay issues. Objectives may include increasing or changing benefits, beginning a variable pay or pay for performance program or instituting a plan to give equity to some or all employees.

Going back to the same groups you used to help you determine key success factors, ask them to list objectives for each key success factor. Next to the objective, write a short description of how you will know if your mission has been successfully accomplished.

What objectives might you set to achieve a particular key success factor? (Answer this with as many responses as you and your managers can generate. Then prioritize.)

Ask Yourself:

☐ Do your objectives fit the key success factor to which they apply?

☐ What objectives might you set to achieve a particular key success factor?

☐ Are the objectives realistic and within the time frame allotted?

☐ If you completed all of the objectives, would you feel you have accomplished that key factor for success?

☐ If you accomplished all of the objectives under each category, would you assure your company's success?

Corporate Objectives Worksheet #1
Finance

Key Success Factor # __1__	
Objectives	**How we will define success**
# __1-1__	
# __1-2__	
# __1-3__	

Key Success Factor # __2__	
Objectives	**How we will define success**
# __2-1__	
# __2-2__	
# __2-3__	

Key Success Factor # __3__	
Objectives	**How we will define success**
# __3-1__	
# __3-2__	
# __3-3__	

Corporate Objectives Worksheet #2
Marketing and Product Development

Key Success Factor # __1__

	Objectives	How we will define success
# __1-1__		
# __1-2__		
# __1-3__		

Key Success Factor # __2__

	Objectives	How we will define success
# __2-1__		
# __2-2__		
# __2-3__		

Key Success Factor # __3__

	Objectives	How we will define success
# __3-1__		
# __3-2__		
# __3-3__		

Corporate Objectives Worksheet #3
Sales and Customer Service

Key Success Factor # __1__

	Objectives	How we will define success
# __1-1__		
# __1-2__		
# __1-3__		

Key Success Factor # __2__

	Objectives	How we will define success
# __2-1__		
# __2-2__		
# __2-3__		

Key Success Factor # __3__

	Objectives	How we will define success
# __3-1__		
# __3-2__		
# __3-3__		

Corporate Objectives Worksheet #4
Operations and Human Resources

Key Success Factor # __1__	
Objectives	**How we will define success**
# __1-1__	
# __1-2__	
# __1-3__	
Key Success Factor # __2__	
Objectives	**How we will define success**
# __2-1__	
# __2-2__	
# __2-3__	
Key Success Factor # __3__	
Objectives	**How we will define success**
# __3-1__	
# __3-2__	
# __3-3__	

Action Plans

Once determined, objectives must be set into motion by more specific plans of action. This means narrowing down to the person responsible and monitoring progress by assigning due dates. Action plans are marching orders and very specific directions for how people need to march—and where they need to arrive at the end of the parade.

Conceptually, the worksheet on the next page is extremely simple. The process applies the theory and abstract concepts that color some of the other worksheets in this section in a practical way.

This is the essence of employee participation in the planning process. Some people enjoy the freedom of a blank piece of paper to dream about what they would like to accomplish. Most, however, just want to know that they can make a contribution.

I try to make it clear exactly what I—and my managers—want this exercise to accomplish. Done well, these action plans can become milestones that we use to gauge performance and progress. That goes for individuals, departments and the company as a whole.

In many cases, this is an appropriate part of a person's annual performance and compensation review. In other cases, we use them on a project-specific basis. Because action plans are so straightforward, they're useful in almost any managerial context.

Give each person who works with you all of the material developed thus far (vision, mission, key success factors and corporate objectives) and then encourage each to write his or her own action plans, linking them to specific corporate objectives.

These action items should be discussed with the manager who sets the objectives. They can become part of the employee's personal goals for the year, and compensation decisions can be determined based on the accomplishment of these specific goals.

There are also objectives within a department or involving more than one department that can only be met with a team of people. Pick the team of

Action Plans

Person or Team _____

Date _____

Key Success Factor #	Objective #	Action Items	Measurement	Deadline

people, or ask for volunteers, and give them this worksheet to develop action items as a group.

Some individuals are much more creative verbally than in writing. Encourage people to sit down with peers from other departments to talk through the meaning of each objective and how their individual work can help contribute. Notes taken from these discussions can translate into meaningful action items.

If you establish this process as a credible exercise, your people will tell you things you might not have even considered before. And if you can tie a person's paycheck into what you want them to accomplish, and also make sure they are recognized for their achievements by their peers, you can almost be certain that they will meet the objectives that they themselves have set.

Once action items are set, negotiate deadlines for completion. Before they are finally written, they should be agreed upon between the manager and the employee. Interim deadlines should be set if it is a long or complex project.

Ask Yourself:

- ☐ Do these action items work toward meeting the set objective?

- ☐ If all the action items under a single objective are met, will the *objective* be met?

- ☐ Are these action items clear enough to give employees adequate direction?

- ☐ Is there any ambiguity about what successful accomplishment means?

- ☐ Is the employee/group committed to getting these things done?

- ☐ Does the employee/group think these plans are realistic considering the current workload?

- ☐ Are there adequate resources available to make these action plans possible?

Tactical Plan Circle

The worksheet at the end of this chapter is to be used explicitly as a communication tool. It translates into graphic form the concepts, objectives and goals you've set out in other exercises.

Pulling together all of the elements from this chapter, we can visually show how each section draws from the previous to make up our tactical plan. It compares different exercises in relation to one another and their overall importance in the management process.

This is a powerful tool for communicating all of the pieces of the planning cycle to your people and for letting them see where their work fits into the whole scheme.

Front-line workers often complain that they're not told where and how their efforts fit into the company as a whole. That feeling can be a major disincentive to effective work and innovation. Take every chance you can to help your coworkers understand their positions in the company.

Colorful, eye-catching visual communication is inspiring and exciting. In my experience, the use of creative graphics helps represent important business concepts. I've tried a number of different methods—glass jars and beads, toy horses on a track and even old-fashioned thermometer graphs.

But the best way to use a graphic is to compare statistics or trends that don't always leap to mind as relevant but, together, shed insight and understanding on a key business function.

The advantage of this graphic is that it tells everyone where he or she fits in the planning process—usually something companies, especially big ones, keep trapped in the board room.

Taking the information developed from the previous worksheets, enlarge the page that follows until it is large enough to write in, and use it to map out your tactics for implementation. A wall-sized circle, posted in a common area, is a very effective means of communication on these important areas.

Use your imagination to add color and graphics as appropriate to broadcast your direction to everyone, everyday. Encourage people to study the chart—and even have employees and managers cross off items that have been completed. Date items at company-wide meetings. Celebrate each of these significant events.

Keeping several years of these circles in a conference room will help remind people of how much they have accomplished.

Ask Yourself:

☐ Looking at your circle, do you have a sense of a team pulling in one direction? Do any of the items you see contradict each other?

☐ Does this look like a year's worth of work? Are all of the items significant and meaningful?

☐ Are you excited by the work this represents? Does this circle help you imagine how you will feel when projects are completed?

☐ Is this document posted in a place where people will find themselves and mentally review their progress (and that of their peers) every day?

Tactical Plan Circle

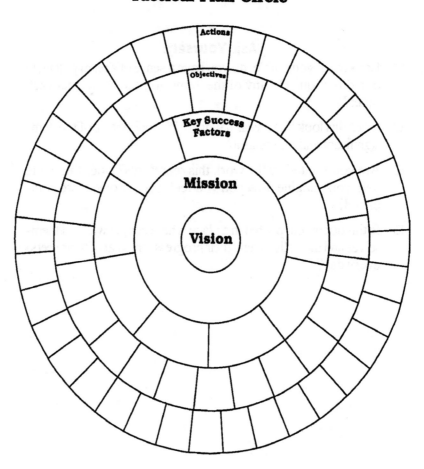

CHAPTER 3:
FINANCIAL PROJECTIONS

One of the most tedious and grueling parts of running a small business is budgeting. People hate budgets. Some hate it so much that they run their business using their daily bank balance as their only financial tool. Some people do well for years in this manner. But if you don't budget formally, you probably do so informally. You know how much it costs to make your products, and what profit margins you need to pay the bills. And you have a pretty good idea of what your company is worth.

Most people resist the notion that they can benefit from good budgeting—until they try it.

Then they learn that budgeting takes some of the hazard out of business by minimizing the guesswork that comes with winging it. Budgeting gives you a blueprint for action. It tells you what to expect and alerts you to trouble when the unexpected happens. It also measures your success; when your business outperforms your projections, you know you're doing well.

This chapter takes you through the basics of budgeting. It shows you how to put together a "bottom-up" budget—that is, an overall budget that reflects the real needs of your business. It presents case studies that show the value of budgeting to a young business and to the business facing a crisis. The worksheets in this chapter show you how to analyze your average selling prices, month-to-month unit sales, sales projections, payroll, expenses and overall performance.

The Basics

Profits aren't everything in business; your vision statement probably says nothing about profits. But without profits and their conversion to cash, no business survives long enough to reach its goals.

Fittingly, therefore, almost everything in budgeting stems from the simple formula for determining profit: sales minus expenses. This formula drives business. Profit defines performance, in other words. Everything else is elaboration.

But you prepare budgets *after* you set direction with your vision and mission statements. Like those items, the budget helps get you from the generalities of your business plan to the specifics of day-to-day operations. By setting priorities, the budget makes clear what your finances permit you to do in order to reach your goals. It translates the vision and mission statements into action. As such, it speaks more loudly than words when it comes to separating the important from the unimportant, since it specifies action.

Above all, the budget is a tool for all people who have responsibility for spending money and making money, not just CEOs. The financials you show your directors, investors and lenders don't tell managers what you expect from them and which of their efforts you value most. Your budget does.

Input from Employees

It's an eccentricity of American business that budgets come down from on high, from senior management—particularly from the finance department. The best budgets show the input of employees. They focus on each business function within the company from the bottom up, starting with zero in each column of numbers. They reflect the thinking of the people who know best where the company really spends its money.

Get the input from these people when you put your budgets and projections together. You send a much greater message about the priorities of the company with what you spend your money on than with your vision or mission statements. If you say your company is committed to customer service and then spend little money training or staffing your customer hotlines, but a lot on your corporate facility, employees will know where your real commitment lies.

Senior managers must also understand and have input in the budget's numbers. Allowing others to budget, allows others to freely determine where money is spent. Good budgeting is a highly interactive process. While people may not argue for changes to the mission statement, they will usually argue for changes in allowable spending. Budgets should be drafted, compared to actuals last year, debated for the best use of resources and redrafted as necessary.

Know When To Stop

It is important to spend time creating your budget, but once you finish it, get back to daily business. The most important point is to have something to measure reality against, not to make the budget perfect. Budgeting becomes more realistic as time goes on. Budget 12 months in advance, and if you can, update quarter by quarter to create a rolling 12-month budget. This will enable you to make changes frequently enough to do reasonably accurate budgeting. Don't think too much about the budgeting process in the meantime.

And build some tolerance for variance into your numbers. Your budget stops being accurate the moment you finish it, and when variances occur—and they will—make sure they buy opportunity for your managers to act creatively. While budgets should be designed to create accountability, accountability should be related to the real issues behind the numbers, not the numbers alone.

Remember that finance plays both operational and analytic roles. Some business owners become excessively enamored of quantitative analysis—to the detriment of qualitative analysis. This can lead to problems. Occasionally, when a finance department detects a company-wide difficulty, it can make matters worse by forcing its priorities on other units.

Illinois-based consultant James Morehouse offers a good example. When an internal audit finds too many assets tied up in inventory, "out goes a memo telling all unit managers to cut inventory 25 percent in six months," he says. "But only the hot items move out fast. The rest sit there. When it's all over, inventories are down 10 percent, the CFO declares victory—and the only items left are the ones nobody wants."

Defense Against Risk

Clearly, numbers don't tell the whole story. This leads some entrepreneurs to suspect the value of any process based on detailed guesses projected to points far in the future.

To be sure, projections are guesses. Their value depends on the assumptions used at the onset. The better the assumption, the better the projection. They shouldn't go too far into the future, and they should forecast sales conservatively and costs liberally, showing what you might call a constructive pessimism.

Budgets serve as defensive mechanisms against risk, alerting the organization to problems lying ahead by building on the past. The important thing is to stay in the game. If you have losses and let those losses continue, you will eventually run out of cash. It usually happens slowly—you have a line of credit that you have maxed out or can't pay back. You take longer and longer to pay your bills. You spend a greater percentage of your time stalling creditors and looking for any source of cash. And eventually, if this continues, you come up to a pay day where there isn't enough cash to meet payroll. And that may be your last day in business.

Budgeting exists to forwarn you of that day way in advance. If you budget, you will have plenty of opportunity to make changes in your operations to avoid that day altogether.

Every business experiences periods of growth, and other, much leaner times. Learning the appropriate budgeting and operational strategy for each will keep you in the game.

Where to Start

The easiest way to begin a projection is to map out at least one year—but no more than three years—based on your performance over the same period in the past. If you don't have that much history, start with the projections you made in your business plan, adjusted to actual performance since you opened for business.

Put your expenses into categories (examples follow later in the chapter) that make sense in your business. The most important thing is to define what expenses you want in each of these categories so that you have some consistency for comparing actual numbers with the budget, and can accurately trend the numbers over time.

You will want to budget according to what actual expenses have been in the past, but proactively as well. Determine how much you think is reasonable to spend on office supplies and budget accordingly. You can establish other benchmarks by comparing your expenses with other companies in your industry. If you belong to a trade group, ask it how other members have done relative to their projections. Have they come in over or under their projections? By less than 5 percent? By more than 10? If you have a specific competitor, try to find out how it has done. If all else fails, find out how businesses in your region do in general.

Follow the Money

Knowing where you stand can yield big benefits, as Andrea Totten discovered in running her California-based quilt-making company, Rags to Riches.

She founded the company in 1971, selling quilts and comforters at flea markets and art fairs, but then used a small catalog to generate orders from stores and designers. "[Business] started getting really busy and that's when I decided that I needed to find a direction," she says. "I guess then I didn't think of the word business plan, but I guess now in retrospect that's what it was."

Totten wrote proposals and went to a variety of lenders only to find most of them reluctant to lend to small businesses and some, it seemed, reluctant to lend to women. "Even though I had a house and a car, they wouldn't take them [as collateral]," she says. "Each year they'd say, 'Come back in a year.' Meanwhile, four or five years passed."

Totten resorted to what she ruefully calls "acid based lending"—high interest loans made against accounts receivable by fashion industry lenders called factors. "You sell your receivables," Totten says. "[The loans] were good at the time because they were needed. But they turned out to be too expensive to maintain."

The factors charged 4.5 percent interest—per month. "The only way to beat it is to keep the money going. And it's like the whole fabric industry is factored. So once the business slows down, it's a killer," she says.

A Heavy Load

She persuaded a bank to lend her working capital when her billings passed half a million dollars. "The bank wasn't that bad, about two percent above prime," she says. Still, Totten found herself devoting 20 percent of her cash flow to servicing debt. And she didn't think her bankers valued small-company business; among other things, they frequently changed the terms of her credit line. She paid her loans down as quickly as she could and eventually got out of debt.

"By the time I took classes on how to write [business plans, the instructors assumed that] you sell $20,000 and the next month you have $20,000 in because the people always pay on time. Not true. Receivables don't come in that smoothly, and vendors want money. Your labor, of course, is COD," she says. "I brought in $80,000 in cash, where was it? The business plan was hard to keep to because of the fluctuations of our industry."

In the late 1980s, a number of Totten's competitors went out of business. Trouble plagued the retail industry, too. Stores that had always paid their bills on time now stalled her, stretching her receivables out to $10,000 or

$15,000. Then suddenly they were gone, leaving her with lots of bad debt.

All this led Totten to manage her receivables strictly. "I never let anybody get high enough to ruin me if I lose," she says. "It's kind of like gambling. Don't ever gamble more than you can afford to lose. I look at my receivables and [decide which] people I'll put on COD. If they don't want to buy from me anymore, that's okay because I'm losing money [with them] anyway."

Slow Downsizing

Totten also downsized by attrition, not replacing employees who left. And once she had little or no short-term debt to preoccupy her, she could reassess her market, too. "I said: 'What do I want to do? Do I want to go and look for new business or do I want to better serve the business I have?' And I chose to stay with the stores that were loyal to me and not advertise. I dropped all that."

She was selling to almost 1,000 retailers throughout the country—too many, she thought. She focused on big customers who paid most reliably and cut back doing business with the rest. In the end, she trimmed her customer list by two-thirds but maintained almost the same revenue. "To me, there are two ways to go out of business. One is to have too many orders and the other is to have too few. I used to look at gross sales. But my accountant showed me if I sell $900,000 a year and my profits are higher—that's my success," she says. "Not if I sell a million a year and my profits are down."

She also cut loose her outside sales reps. They took 10 percent commissions and often didn't service the customer well, giving out the wrong information or not knowing the answers to key questions. "So they'd be calling us. I'd be paying two people to do the same job. Now we have our [in-house] reps call and customers fax the orders in. We call back and go over the order with them," she says.

Throughout this restructuring she kept prices steady, protecting her margins. Her strategy translated into stiff terms with her customers. Rags to Riches doesn't give retailers discounts beyond those on its price list. And even those eligible for a discount must display the company's wares prominently.

"It's one thing to get into a new store, but it's another thing to get reorders," she says. In fact, she uses reorder trends as her main diagnostic test for how the company is doing. "If we don't get reorders, then we know that something's wrong. Either the salespeople don't know how to sell [the product] or it's not displayed correctly or it's in the wrong store."

Her final observation about taking control of her company's finances: "Small business people have to keep up with what is happening just as much as a CEO at a huge corporation. If you're not on top of your finances on a real-time basis, you're not going to make it."

Controling Expenses

Andrea Totten grew her business by remaining flexible and by keeping an attentive eye on her market. She controled expenses and reshaped her finances to fit her needs. She learned the value of understanding the impact of finances on her business.

It's good advice. Evaluate your projections regularly, particularly when adding capital to your business, yours or somebody else's. If you have a hunch about the future, follow it—but look for similar surprises in the past and find out what impact they had; don't adjust your financial projections on instinct. Instead, base your new thinking on as much hard evidence as you can gather. Your hunch may tell you that an upturn lies around the corner—but that new market you pursue may trail the overall economy by a year.

The owners of new businesses often review every expense but, as things progress, they back off. They control expenses with budgets and paper trails—i.e., invoices and purchase orders—and make sure that only a few accountable people handle cash.

Spend most of your budgeting time on the big numbers, where most of your money is spent. The major categories will be revenue, payroll, inventory costs, marketing and sales, facility, insurance, computers and others that may be related to your particular business. Here are some good reminders about holding down expenses:

Purchasing. In a small business, put one person—not five or six—in charge of ordering merchandise and using overnight mail services.

Supplies. Make your employees aware of the costs of office supplies; some managers mark the individual cost of each item, such as pens, on the box. Hold your managers responsible for expenses in their departments. Keep an eye out for such ancillary costs as delivery fees. You may spend less to send an hourly worker to pick up supplies.

Travel and entertainment. Scrutinize expenses such as travel and entertainment. Trips should be planned in advance when possible, and made to take advantage of travel discounts, especially some of those now found on the Internet. Make sure that travel and entertainment expenses pay off with increased business.

Insurance. Ask your carriers about safety programming. Consider increasing deductibles for employee health insurance. When sales and profits are down, tell your carrier. You might be able to adjust your coverage—and premiums.

Professional fees. Negotiate fees paid to lawyers and accountants, by the project or the period of time, or even their hourly rate. Also, set caps on what can be spent without specific approval.

Computers and related fees. A great deal of money has been spent in the past few years on personal computers and software, most of it necessary. Set a budget for computer hardware and a separate budget for software and technical support.

Records. Maintain good records and paper trails. Most companies that fail don't have adequate bookkeeping and never know where they stand.

Staying Liquid

Knowing how to slow down spending and collect what others owe you are essential skills in any business. They allow you to access the cash you need to grow or stay in the game.

Accounts payable are the bills that have come in from vendors to whom you owed money. It is often possible to negotiate terms from these vendors that will allow you to hold on to your money longer. For instance, you may be able to pay bills in 45 days instead of the customary 30 (this varies by industry) if you work it out ahead of time.

Accounts receivable are monies that your customers owe you for product already delivered. The object here is to collect this money as quickly as possible.

When a company is facing a financial downturn, one of the first things it does is slow down the paying of its bills. It may be unable to borrow from a bank at that point, so it borrows from its vendors. It is important to know how to do this well, and know when it is being done to you. If you find you need to pay bills late, the most important thing is to maintain communications with your vendors. It would be expensive for them to have to forcibly collect these monies from you, so they will likely be willing to hang in there for some time, as long as you provide them with a plan for repayment. This is particularly important if you need to keep purchasing from them during your financial crisis.

Do not get in the habit of paying your vendors late unless necessary. When it becomes necessary, you will need the track record of a good payment history to convince them to give you extra time. Especially in tight industry niches, word travels about who pays on time and who doesn't. The day may come when you need a favor from a vendor who feels ill-used or when a credit agency down-grades your payment rating.

Coming from the opposite perspective, it is important to know the top (at least) 10 customers who owe you money and to track their payment habits. You are more likely to be paid if you maintain regular communication with them, and they need your services on an ongoing basis. You should specify a maximum amount of credit you are willing to extend to each customer, and watch carefully any customers at the upper end of that limit. Don't loan more than you can afford to lose.

A Sharp Point

A sudden change in business fortunes requires some thinking about the impact of the numbers you study on your business and its future. Sometimes the numbers yield the keys to keeping a good company afloat, as Florida-based pencil maker Dixon Ticonderoga Co. discovered in the early 1990s.

Dixon Ticonderoga, the company that makes school and office supply products, hadn't reported a profit since 1988 and hadn't paid a dividend since 1989. In 1990, losses peaked at $5 million on sales of $82 million. Best known for its yellow Ticonderoga pencils, it also sells children's crayons, paints, rubber bands, artist's materials, felt-tip markers and specialty crayons. Unlike its better-capitalized competitors Empire Berol USA and Faber-Castell Corp., Dixon Ticonderoga makes virtually every product it sells. This runs up expenses but allows the company to control quality and scheduling tightly.

CEO Gino Pala considered the situation serious enough to call for a new business plan. He felt the need for deep changes in the way the company did business, particularly in the way it managed assets, structured operations and used budgets.

Pala's team put together a business plan that projected sales and profit out for three years. The effort, he says, stemmed from a question asked by an hourly production worker during a tour of an Ohio plant. The worker asked Pala whether the company would survive its financial problems.

Pala cut middle management and closed two factories. Real estate in Canada and Florida went on the auction block to bolster liquidity. The company established a central R&D lab to shepherd new products to market.

A Key Problem

The company attacked a key problem—liquidity in the first half of its fiscal year. The critical back-to-school season came during the second half; Pala wanted to keep the first half close to breakeven, to maximize second-half profits. He launched a major cost-cutting drive, reducing first-half operating losses by almost 80 percent by the mid-1990s.

Pala and his managers monitored expenditures directly. They applied cost-evaluation to justify every major bill the company paid; by 1992, Pala says, the company could explain the impact on sales of every payment over $1,000.

The company made a big push into the expanding colored pencils market; its research showed an annual growth rate of 12 to 14 percent in this market. To improve its mastery of inventory and time management, the company started communicating with major customers via computer. It changed its marketing approaches in an effort to address the needs of such mega-stores as Office Depot, Bizmart and other national office wholesalers.

"We identified our key customers—something we hadn't done in a long time," Pala says. "Doing that answered most of our big questions. Once that was done, we knew what we had to look for and what we could just let go. Knowing what's important and what's not is the most important key to writing and using good budgets."

As Pala cut costs, the company looked to expand its market share around the globe. It hired new management for its United Kingdom operations and expanded its ties to a unit in Mexico, yielding "the ability to manufacture labor and energy-intensive items at a significant cost advantage," Pala said.

Dixon Ticonderoga's turnaround efforts paid off. For 1998 it had record revenues of almost $125 million and a growth rate of 18 percent for the past five years. It also began a major repurchase of its own shares in 1999 showing the confidence its management had about its future.

Sharing Information

The hourly worker who asked Gino Pala whether Dixon Ticonderoga would survive posed a fundamental question for business owners—whether to share information about company finances and how much. Progressive managers make it a priority to educate staff on company finances. They make budgets widely accessible, at least within the confines of company facilities.

Still, it scares many managers—even progressive ones—to be open with the financials. As a rule we feel uneasy sharing money matters under any circumstances, considering them wholly personal.

And some companies operate in such competitive fields that they risk a great deal if they bandy about their financial information.

But in most companies, you don't endanger your position by sharing at least the most functional financial information with your coworkers. People are sometimes more sophisticated about money than you think; your employees may surprise you with suggestions like the one about inventory that came from one of my hourly employees.[3] In any case, they may welcome your openness as a sign of trust. I see sharing financial information as a *quid pro quo*. I expect my employees to give me their best, and in exchange, I think they have a right to see how their efforts pay off.

A Caveat

Sharing information with employees doesn't mean loosening the reins on financial controls and checks and balances to prevent errors and theft. It is estimated that employee theft may cause U.S. businesses as much as $100 billion each year. Discuss with your CPA the best methods you can use to prevent fraud and embezzlement. I found the following essential both for my own peace of mind and the protection of my employees:

- Mail should be opened and checks received should be listed on a form by someone other than the bookkeeper.

- Checks should be marked "For Deposit Only" and deposited the same day received.

[3]See Introduction

- Purchase orders or other documentation must be required for every check made out. Approval requirements should be set depending on the size of the check.

- Bank statements must be reconciled monthly by someone outside the accounting department. I used to have statements sent to my home instead of the office.

- The same person should not be buying and receiving inventory.

- It is always a red flag if employees in accounting or who do purchasing never take vacations.

The Bottom Line

You can get away with doing your finances in your head for a while, but when your payroll grows beyond a handful of workers, you need to put things on paper.

Successful companies use their budgeting to identify specific, realistic and quantifiable goals. Budgets bring order to the task of pursuing those goals. First, you identify a revenue or sales objective for the year, using the worksheets in Chapter 2. Then, you identify the tasks necessary to reach that objective. That done, you explore the costs and budget for them, outlining the time and resources you must commit in order to reach the goal. The budget quantifies your plan in dollars.

It also tells your managers and employees what you value as an owner or manager. Money sends a clear message about your priorities. Budgets act as a language for communicating your goals to others.

Your budgets send clear messages outside the organization, too. Lenders and investors don't do business with people whose position they can't understand. They want to see budgets for at least a year in advance and often more. They want cash flow projections and a comprehensible plan for making steady profits.

But remember that you don't win when bankers or investors give you money. You win when you pay them off. For new businesses, the first order of business is to pay off lenders. The surest way to do this is to identify basic financial factors and measure them, so that you can make mid-course corrections.

It takes work, but don't let financial analysis and reporting bog you down. Finance doesn't set policy except *in extremis*. It carries out policy. If you lock into budgets so strict that you can't make monthly adjustments, bad things are bound to happen.

In short, don't keep your budgets and financial projections in a drawer. Use them to chart the implementation of your strategies. There's no guarantee that careful budgeting and financial analysis will bring the success you want. But without them, failure becomes more likely.

Scrutinize every potential risk that your business faces. That means looking at—and sometimes looking beyond—the bottom line.

Creating a Budget

At our company, we created a Budget Notebook each year that documented every expense item, including which suppliers we had used and general ledger numbers to correctly categorize each expense.

The following page represents an index for our budget notebook. The categories in bold type are section topics and have their own sections. Each line item listed has its own page. Each company will have its own additional items, but these are the main categories that are almost universal.

The importance of complete documentation in your budgeting process cannot be overemphasized:

First, the budgeting exercise in this book makes you really analyze your sales projections and expenses in detail. It doesn't allow you to pass over any item.

Second, it tells your accounting department how you want items categorized for reporting purposes. You may wonder why rents are so high on

Budget Index

	General Ledger Account Numbers
Sales Projections	
Cost of Goods Sold	▓▓▓▓▓▓▓▓▓▓▓▓
Materials purchased	
Salaries & wages	
Production supplies	
Temporary help	
Shipping supplies	
Mailing & shipping	
Sales & Marketing Expenses	▓▓▓▓▓▓▓▓▓▓▓▓
Salaries	
Sales commissions	
Direct mail	
Advertising	
Publicity	
Consulting	
Other sales & marketing expense	
Overhead Expenses	▓▓▓▓▓▓▓▓▓▓▓▓
Personnel	▓▓▓▓▓▓▓▓▓▓▓▓
Salaries	
Bonuses	
Payroll taxes	
Group life & health insurance	
Workers' comp. insurance	
Employee benefit plans	
Officers' salaries	
Employment expense	
Training	
Temporary help	
Facilities	▓▓▓▓▓▓▓▓▓▓▓▓
Rents	
Property tax	
Repairs & maintenance	
Utilities	
Property & liability insurance	
Administration	▓▓▓▓▓▓▓▓▓▓▓▓
Accounting services	
Automobiles	
Bank charges	

Chapter 3: Financial Projections

General Ledger Account Numbers

Computer supplies	
Contributions	
Depreciation & amortization	
Dues & subscriptions	
Legal services	
Licenses	
Miscellaneous	
Office supplies	
Other professional services	
Retirement plans	
Telephone	
Travel	
Income Taxes	

your reports. It may be because accounting thinks you want equipment rents expense reported here, while you think accounting allocates this expense to repairs and maintenance. This way everyone is clear on which expense goes where.

Third, it will convince your employees, like nothing else, that you mean business about really scrutinizing what is being spent.

I'm convinced that there is only one way to start to review your expenses and project your sales: from the bottom up. And in writing.

I hope it goes without saying that the number crunching part of the budgeting process can and should be done by computer. The reason for putting the interim and final product in a notebook is to allow for easy access and discussion at meetings, and for reference during the year. It makes it a much more accessible document for employees.

Spreadsheets can be set up by department on a computer network, giving each manager a password for access to his or her department's section only. These can automatically be added to the total company worksheet, so that changes will total immediately.

Many companies project expenses by increasing each expense item by a regular annual percentage or budget as a percentage of sales. In contrast, a bottom-up method forces you essentially to start over each year.

This allows you more flexibility to do things like reducing expenses. When you carefully analyze the checks you write, you may find you're paying for things you aren't using. Especially for ongoing commitments such as maintenance agreements, annual review is essential.

Try to use the "miscellaneous" line item as little as possible. I never budget for anything other than petty cash in this category so it will not become a catch-all for items accounting cannot otherwise categorize.

Done well, the budget notebook can be the one place to find all the answers. You can keep copies of contracts in this notebook to show expense commitments you have made for periods of time that may be beyond the current year.

Lastly, this kind of notebook helps employees understand how the company's money is being spent. Employees sometimes overestimate—significantly—how much the owner or manager takes out of a business. They assume that if you take in $3 million in revenue, the owner is taking home $2 million. The notebook shows them how much money it takes to make payroll, pay insurance premiums, pay rent, etc.

Set up your notebook in a three-ring binder first—don't worry about what you'll put in it. Prepare the dividers and have one blank sheet of paper for each item with its title on the top. To begin writing, start with the easiest items first, usually some recurring, consistent expenses. For example, how much do you pay in rent each month? Add to this any information you need regarding your lease, such as the starting and ending dates and when increases occur. This is a good time to review your lease and look for any hidden costs that will need to be a part of your budget.

Each line item has several general ledger account numbers associated with it. These general ledger numbers are used by your accounting staff to allocate every item for which the company writes checks. By looking at each of the expenditures in each general ledger account number, you can do budgeting from the bottom up. Ask your accounting department to add your general ledger numbers to the right side of this sheet.

The budget notebook starts with sales projections and we focus on them in the first few worksheets later in this chapter. Your sales divider should be followed by the completed Average Price Per Product worksheet, the Unit Sales by Product worksheet, and the Dollar Sales Projections by Product and by Month worksheets. These will give you a system to calculate conservative expectations of sales by which you can realistically budget expenses.

We have four other sections that call for dividers in our notebook:

Cost of Goods Sold—the expenses incurred in making your product;

Sales and Marketing Expenses—what it costs you to sell your product;

Overhead Expenses—most of the other expenses incurred in operating an office; and

Income Taxes—we don't discuss estimating taxes in this book, but you should have a section in your notebook for tax planning and discuss this with your CPA.

In addition, we have a section for the balance sheet budget, which includes major capital expenditures and other items beyond the scope of this annual budgeting process. But they must be considered.

Ask Yourself:

☐ Are your expense categories all encompassing? Would all of your supplier's services fit into some category?

☐ Will the categories you have chosen be meaningful in decision making?

☐ Do some of these categories house too many different types of items so it won't be clear what the category means?

☐ Does your budgeting process include most if not all employees? Do you feel certain you have captured all your real expenses?

☐ Have you reviewed supplier contracts or other agreements to capture all costs and look for cost reduction possibilities?

Average Selling Price per Product

To begin to project your sales for the year, it is essential to know how much you are selling of each unit of product now. This worksheet considers pricing issues, across all of your product lines, in detail.

This is critical if you discount your prices for volume or other criteria. You may think your prices are close to retail, but the average price may be at a deeper discount than you think.

This worksheet is useful in making pricing decisions. In some industries, there are standard discounts and pricing schedules required by retailers from wholesalers.

If you know you must make at least $10 per unit to be profitable, and the discount required by retailers is 50 percent, you must set your retail price at $20—at least.

The trend in average price per product may also give some important signs about your business and your industry. If the average selling price drops consistently from year to year (as is the case, for example, with computer software), you will have to become much more efficient in production in order to remain profitable.

In addition, this worksheet gives you valuable information about what your customers are willing to pay for your products. This kind of information can be used with the marketing tools we talk about elsewhere in this book. After calculating the average selling price per product, compare this to your largest customers. Are they buying way below this number? Are some of your larger customers willing to buy at a number higher than this?

This approach to determining price per unit may be too basic for companies with complex product lines (though the theory behind price per unit measurement remains useful). But it will work in many cases.

To calculate your average price per product, list your products in column A and their total sales volume in column B. In column C, list how many units were sold of each. In column D, list the selling price for each unit of the product. To compute the average price per unit in column E, divide column B by column C. For F, the average discount from the selling price, divide column E by column D. Complete this exercise for at least two years' worth of information.

Ask Yourself:

☐ Has your average price per unit decreased or increased over the past two years?

☐ How have your selling prices increased or decreased over the same period of time?

Business Plans to Game Plans

Average Selling Price per Product

A Product	B Total $ Sales	C # of Units Sold	D Selling Price $ per Unit	E Average Price $ per Unit (B÷C)	F % of Selling Pricee (E÷D)

❑ Are discounts—as a percentage—about the same over the last two years or have they stayed the same? Do you have to give up a larger percentage of total revenues over time?

❑ Can your discounting policy be changed to encourage purchase of higher margin products?

❑ Is one customer large enough to be responsible for a sizeable drop in average price per product?

Unit Sales by Product

It is important to begin any series of sales projections with what your actual unit sales were last year. Sales dollars may be increasing year to year because of price increases, while unit volume may actually be decreasing.

The number of things that you sell—regardless of price or terms—reflects the underlying strengths of your business. If unit sales aren't increasing, then you aren't growing in real terms.

Keep the actual numbers that come from these worksheets over time. All products have life-cycles. You will see which products have consistent sales, and which have increasing or decreasing sales. Generally, a handful of products has unit sales much greater than expected (although dollar sales might be right on target, or even below expectations). Most have sales slightly below our usually optimistic projections.

Unit sales are a much better method of measuring real growth than are dollar sales. Dollar sales can be impacted by such things as price changes and additional charges. Decreasing unit sales provide an early warning signal that can be addressed now rather than later—when dollar volume sales begin to drop as well.

List all the types of products you sold last year in the far left column of the worksheet. Then tabulate the actual number of units you sold for each type of product by month. Add the total units by product in the first shaded column. In the last column, divide this number by 12 to get your average unit sales by month.

Business Plans to Game Plans

Unit Sales By Product   ☐ Actuals for this year

PRODUCT	1 Jan.	2 Feb.	3 Mar.	4 April	5 May	6 June
Totals						

☐ **Projections for this year**   ☐ **Actuals for this year**

7 July	8 Aug.	9 Sept.	10 Oct.	11 Nov.	12 Dec.	Unit Sales Year- to-date	Avg. Unit Sales by Mo.*

*Divide total year-to-date unit sales by current month number.

Now do this worksheet a second time to project the number of units you expect to sell this year. Project as conservatively as possible. If you do not have a specific reason to expect an increase, use last years' average numbers as a projection. In some products you probably expect a decrease. There will also be new products to add that you may not have had last year. Factor these differences into your projections.

You can also apply a percentage increase to the number of units sold last year to get a projection for this year, although this tends to be less accurate than estimating what you will sell month-to-month based on marketing efforts.

Finally, this worksheet can be used to monitor how close your actual unit sales are to your projections by adding the actual numbers to a third blank worksheet.

Ask Yourself:

☐ Are unit sales cyclical as evidenced by sharp increases in certain months or seasons?

☐ Are unit increases due to particular marketing efforts?

☐ Are unit sales obviously affected by particular accounts' buying patterns?

☐ Are new products doing as well as expected as soon as expected?

☐ Have any products sales dwindled during the year or from the past year?

Dollar Sales Projections by Product

This worksheet helps you project—conservatively—the dollar sales using unit projections by product using an average selling price from the prior year.

It is important for the morale of the company to be aggressive in marketing and to have high expectations of the sales growth you want to achieve.

But save these high hopes for your sales meetings. The budgeting process considers both sales and expenses. If you project a 20 percent increase in sales for the purpose of determining your profit picture, you may allow yourself to increase your expenses by more than you should.

While the company is busy looking at what it is spending, the sales and marketing people must be busy looking at what the expected sales are.

Take a very conservative approach to sales projections. Base them as much as possible on what actually happened last year, both in terms of real unit sales and your actual average selling prices. Factor in any price increases and expected unit increases very carefully.

In virtually all but the most disciplined companies, if sales are up, people ease up on the expense reins and the horse runs free. Almost every employee can find something he or she would like to have to improve his or her lot. If money appears to be no object, people will ask for more than they really need—including everything from office furniture to computer software.

Since the most realistic sales projections are done by looking not at dollars, but at units sold, we begin with the unit sales number from the previous worksheet. The number of units you project will be sold is then multiplied by the average price you got for the product last year to get an idea of what sales dollars the product would be expected to bring in this year.

It is also important to factor in any price increases, but be very conservative in doing so. If you increase your selling price by 10 percent, often you don't increase your discounted price to high-volume purchasers by an equal amount. In this case you might want to only factor in a five percent increase in the average price.

To get a total, multiply columns B, C and D together. The shaded box at bottom should be your total expected dollar sales for the entire year.

Ask Yourself:

☐ Have you reviewed profitability and market factors to consider price increases?

Dollar Sales Projections By Product

A Product	B[1] Units Sales By Product	C[2] Average Price Per Product

[1]From *Unit Sales By Product* worksheet
[2]From *Average Price Per Product* worksheet

D Projected Price Increases (%)	Projected $ Sales (B x C x D)

☐ Are projected sales substantially greater or less than actual sales from last year?

☐ Are sales projections particularly aggressive for some products and not for others? Do these differences accurately reflect the positions of various products in their sales cycles?

☐ Are there other significant sources of income not taken into account by product sales (such as shipping and handling)?

☐ Is there any other information, such as the possible loss of a major customer, that needs to be factored into sales projections?

Dollar Sales Projections by Month

This worksheet takes the dollar sales projections developed on the prior worksheet and allocates them by month, looking at how sales came in by month during the previous year.

It is important to know when we expect the sales to be booked. For most companies, sales are recorded upon shipment of the company's product.

Filling in this sheet with your actual sales figures from last year will allow you to see if any of your products are seasonal. Even if sales of your products generally don't appear to have any dramatic fluctuations from month to month, certain products may. This might signal a particular buying segment that orders at a particular time of year. Knowing this may help you spend your marketing dollars for this buying group at the right time.

For the purpose of accurate projections, it is important to run this worksheet twice.

First, use actual numbers from the last full year to get the percentages that are calculated at the bottom of the page. These numbers show what percentage of the total sales was made each month of the previous 12 months. The total in the box at the bottom right should be 100 percent.

List your products in the left-hand column. List your actual dollar sales by product for each of the last 12 months. Total the numbers, month by month, at the bottom of the page. Using these total dollar figures, divide the total dollars by month by the total dollars in the shaded box at the bottom right corner. Enter these percentages by month at the bottom of each column.

For your second calculation, use the totals and percentages you just calculated at the bottom of the first Dollar Sales Projections by Product worksheet, to make sales projections. This time, enter the total dollars by product that you calculated in the previous worksheet (from Dollar Sales Projections by Product) in the far right column of the worksheet, and total at the bottom. Then enter the percentages by month at the bottom of the page from the percentages done on the worksheet showing the actuals from last year. Multiply the number in the total column by the percentage at the bottom to get a number to fill in each box. This will give you an expected dollar sales volume by month.

Illustrating this data graphically (a simple bar chart works well) will increase its impact.

Ask Yourself:

☐ What effect does seasonality have on sales and cash flow?

☐ How do debt services and other major financial commitments coincide with or run counter to the annual sales cycle? How will this affect your cash flow?

☐ Will profit margin decrease substantially because of variable costs coming into play during certain times of the year?

☐ Can marketing efforts be adjusted to smooth out erratic cyclical and seasonal sales patterns?

☐ Will you require a line of credit or some other borrowing mechanism if cash flow isn't adequate to meet expenses during certain times of the year? Is that borrowing mechanism ready?

Dollar Sales Projections By Month

Product	Jan.	Feb.	Mar.	April	May
Product	$	$	$	$	$
% By Month	%	%	%	%	%

☐ **Actuals (last year)**
☐ **Projections (this year)**

June	July	Aug.	Sept.	Oct.	Nov.	Dec.	Total*
$	$	$	$	$	$	$	$
%	%	%	%	%	%	%	100%

*From *Dollar Sales Projections By Product* worksheet for this year only

Expense Budgeting

This process gives you a format for writing down and tracking anticipated expense items. It also allows you to compare last year's anticipated and actual numbers for the same group of expenses.

This worksheet is an example of what a budget notebook page might look like. I've provided a sample of a page called "rents." Rents might include office building leases, parking, warehousing and equipment rentals. Start by listing, at the bottom of the page, what the budget and actual numbers were for the previous year. This will give you an idea of what the expense figure for this year might be and whether there is a tendency to over- or under-budget for this item.

The rents category may include several general ledger accounts—office space rental, equipment rental, warehouse rentals, etc. For each of these general ledger account numbers, your accounting department should have a standard list of vendors to whom they often write checks. Ask to see this standard list on a regular basis.

Budgeting should be a participative process. Doing it alone defeats the purpose. Teams should be given the responsibility to analyze last year's bills and project expenditures by category and vendor this year. Especially once you have been through the process a year or two, teams should report annually to you on ways to reduce these expenses. Management's role during the process should be limited to making final decisions on approving expenditures, putting it all together and—hopefully—getting the desired profit picture.

First, list the type of item on each blank sheet, and next to it list the vendor of that item. Lastly, make an estimate of how much you think you will spend on that item this year. This estimate can be made by looking at how much you spent last year and making an educated guess as to whether this will go up or down. You can also often get a close to actual number if the item is based on a contractual agreement and doesn't often vary. Be sure to consider automatic price increase clauses and other hidden costs frequently overlooked.

Sample Expense Budget Page

20 ___

RENTS

Main Building	ABC Properties	$ 196,806

($16,198/mo. increases 3% on 8/1/04)

Parking	Parking Lots Inc.	$ 480

(12 spaces at $40/mo.)

Warehouse	SuperStorage	$ 2,400

($200/mo.)

Equipment Rentals

Postage meter rental	Pitney/Bowes	$ 835

($412.50 twice a year, due 1/1 and 7/1)

Copy machines	Xerox	$ 4,272

($356/mo. expires 4/4/05)

Telephone	Bell Communications	$ 14,628

($1,219/mo. expires 7/1/07)

TOTAL: $ 219,421

Budget last year: $ 195,008

Actual last year: $ 201,962

Wherever possible in our budget, we've listed the important financial points of the lease to make this process easier next year, and to let the accounting department know if these payments are expected to increase, stop or decrease at any point during the year.

Ask Yourself:

- ☐ Have you captured all important expense items in the worksheet?

- ☐ Are your preliminary estimates significantly over or under the actual numbers for last year?

- ☐ Are explanatory notes understandable to everyone?

- ☐ Are there any items that you find you are no longer using?

- ☐ Are there any numbers that seem out of proportion to the value of the service you are paying for?

- ☐ Look at total amounts paid to various vendors during your last full year. Will this year be about the same as last? Is there an automatic increase to any of these expenses?

- ☐ Do you plan to use less of a given product or service next year?

- ☐ Do you always pay a specific amount for a given product or service each month, or does it vary by the quantity used?

- ☐ Are there new vendors you're negotiating with now that you plan to begin using in the near future? How will they compare with existing expense items?

Insurance Policy and Payments Schedules

The goal of the two worksheets on the upcoming pages is to have all of the information pertaining to insurance policies summarized on one page and to have the payments listed by month on a second page.

The insurance worksheets will help you categorize insurance by type (also essential for categorizing your costs). They'll also help you remember when to renew your policies and, considering your other expenditures, help you decide when it is convenient for you to pay for your insurance premiums over time.

Insurance costs—and, therefore, savings—can be great. The cost of insurance will go up and down depending on sales, total assets, total payroll, etc. Accurate budgeting may work to keep premium dollars under control.

Initially, you might choose to have your insurance agent or broker complete the worksheets for you.

I find it essential for planning another one of the larger expenditures faced by every business, such as payroll, to have all of the information pertaining to my insurance policies summarized in one location.

The first worksheet—the Insurance Policy Schedule—lists the major types of insurance most businesses choose (or are required) to carry on the left. The blank spaces are for you to fill in the types of policies you have that might be specific to your industry (for instance, we always carried a publishers' liability policy).

Next, list the carrier (insurance company), the policy number, the expiration date (or in the case of life insurance, when the policy started), the total annual premium, policy limits and deductibles and an explanation of when the policies must be paid.

Keeping copies of this worksheet from year to year will allow you to see how much your insurance costs are increasing. Show these to your agent or broker, and ask for explanations.

Taking information from the Insurance Policy Schedule, the second worksheet—the Insurance Payments Schedule—will help you know when payments for each insurance policy come due. This will help you in planning your cash requirements.

It is important to note that any significant item of your expenses could be planned out like your insurance payments on this same type of worksheet.

Insurance Policy Schedule

Type	Carrier	Limits	Deductible	Policy #	Expiration (or policy inception)	Yearly Premium
Insurance - L & H*						
Medical						
Dental						
Disability						
Life						
Travel Accident						
Insurance - P & C**						
Commercial Package (property - liability)						
Commercial Atuo						
Commercial Umbrella						
Employee Dishonesty						
Ins. - Workers' Comp.						
Workers' Comp.						
Ins. - Officer's Life						
					Total	
					Grand Total	

*Life and Health
**Property and Casualty

Ask Yourself:

☐ Could you carry higher deductibles to reduce premiums?

☐ Could you self-insure any portion of your insurance?

☐ Are your limits of liability adequate to cover all of your assets?

☐ Do you have all of the types of insurance your business requires?

☐ Are there ways to reduce premiums by shopping for new carriers?

☐ How will changes in payroll change your workers' comp. insurance classifications and premiums?

Go to worksheet on the following page   →

Insurance Payments Schedule

Type	Carrier	Jan.	Feb.	Mar.	April	May
Total By Month:						

June	July	Aug.	Sept.	Oct.	Nov.	Dec.	Total

Payroll Projections

Payroll is one piece of most budgets that not everyone can access. This makes it difficult to study for cost reduction as openly as you might any other budget item.

This worksheet will accurately project and document payroll—the largest area of expense for most companies.

It is important to project payroll accurately, not only because it is a significant expense in and of itself, but also because of its direct impact on many other expense categories. Payroll taxes, workers' comp insurance, life and disability insurance and retirement plan expenses generally all fluctuate with changes in payroll.

To calculate payroll, ask each manager to determine his department's head count and payroll costs on the next worksheet. The worksheet gives columns for each employee's current salary (times a number of months) plus a column for a salary increase (times the number of months the higher salary will be in effect).

Adding the numbers in the last column gives you the total compensation of each department's employees for the year. Add below the actual payroll for that department last year.

Totaling the shaded box at the bottom right of each department worksheet will give you the total company payroll.

Payroll is rarely, if ever, reduced, except in crises. Employees never expect their salaries to be static. They generally expect their compensation to increase—at least once a year. These increases rarely respond to real productivity increases. They're part of an entitlement employees feel about their jobs, which most assume include a higher salary and greater benefits with each passing year.

Because of the always-growing nature of payrolls, many companies are experimenting with progressive compensation plans like performance-based pay. But, regardless of how you determine what you pay your employees, payroll must be projected to get an accurate profit picture.

Ask Yourself:

- ☐ Are some departments' payrolls increasing more quickly than others? Is this due to additions to staff or pay increases? Is this in line with your overall growth plans?

- ☐ Are your payroll dollars going to the areas you wish to emphasize?

- ☐ Are managers realistic about the increases they want to give?

- ☐ How much has your total payroll increased this year? In dollars? As a percentage? How will this affect other expenses?

- ☐ Is your compensation competitive for your industry?

- ☐ Do you check at least annually for internal equity in your compensation system?

Go to worksheet on the following page   ➔

Payroll Projections

Department _____

Employee Number	Employee Name	Current Monthly Salary (if hourly wage, convert to monthly*)	x # of mos.	= total at current salary

Formula to convert hourly rate to monthly rate is: hourly rate x 173.3 (example $10.00hr. x 173.3 = $1733.mo.)

> *Please use pencil.*
> *Round figures to the nearest dollar.*

next Salary increase (date)	x % inc.	Future Salary (if hourly wage, convert to monthly*)	X of mos.	= total at new salary	TOTAL COMPENSATION (total shaded columns)
			TotalForDepartment		

ActualforDepartmentLastYear

Payroll by Classification by Month

This worksheet combines information provided by each manager and divides it by classifications relevant to how you want to look at your actual payroll expenses.

By breaking these sections of total payroll out separately, you can get clearer measurements of how much it costs to make your product, how much it costs to sell it, and what some of your administrative (overhead) costs are.

In addition, you should want to look at how payroll is spread out over time. Most entrepreneurs know exactly when they need to cover their payroll. It's hard for most employees to understand, but if your payroll is $1 million a year (and a company of 35 people can easily have that), the company sends out about $40,000 worth of paychecks every two weeks.

My company paid employees every other Friday, which came out to 26 paychecks a year. This generally meant that employees received three paychecks in June and December, and two in the other months of the year. Accordingly, our payroll on a cash basis was higher in June and December than during the other months. This becomes important to know if June is your lowest sales month.

Use your Payroll Projections worksheets by department to fill out this worksheet, employee by employee. Be careful to put their pay increases into the right months. Classify each employee in one of four ways:

(1) *Cost of Goods Sold* (salaries & wages): the payroll of those employees who contribute directly to the production of the product.

(2) *Sales and Marketing Expense* (salaries): salaries and commissions of sales and marketing employees.

(3) *Overhead Expense* (salaries): all other employees, not otherwise categorized.

(4) *Officers' Salaries*: the owners and officers of the company should be categorized separately.

Sum up the columns for the grand totals at the bottom of the page.

Payroll By Classification By Month

Cost of Goods Sold (salaries & wages)

Employee	Monthly Salary	Jan.	Feb.	Mar.	April	May	June	July	Aug.	Sept.	Oct.	Nov.	Dec.	Totals
Totals														

Sales and Marketing Expense (salaries)

Employee	Monthly Salary	Jan.	Feb.	Mar.	April	May	June	July	Aug.	Sept.	Oct.	Nov.	Dec.	Totals
Totals														

Overhead Expense (salaries)

Employee	Monthly Salary	Jan.	Feb.	Mar.	April	May	June	July	Aug.	Sept.	Oct.	Nov.	Dec.	Totals
Totals														

Officers' Salaries

Employee	Monthly Salary	Jan.	Feb.	Mar.	April	May	June	July	Aug.	Sept.	Oct.	Nov.	Dec.	Totals
Totals														

Grand Totals	Jan.	Feb.	Mar.	April	May	June	July	Aug.	Sept.	Oct.	Nov.	Dec.	

- ☐ Do some months require significantly more dollars to meet payroll than others?

- ☐ Is it possible to stagger pay increases throughout the year?

- ☐ Are salary dollars spent making and selling the products, or is a lot more spent on administrative overhead?

- ☐ During what months are incentive bonuses and other special compensation paid? How are different departments affected by these items?

- ☐ Is your projected head-count higher or lower than last year? How will that influence other expenses?

Total Company Projections

This exercise pulls together on one page all the items gathered in the budget notebook and looks overall at your profit picture.

Categorizing your expenses this way is important to begin to look at your overall profit picture as a number you can control.

From the information gathered in the budget notebook, you can begin to analyze your profit picture by putting your numbers in six major categories as follows:

(1) Sales

(2) Cost of goods sold

(3) Sales and marketing expenses

(4) Overhead expenses (including administration, personnel, facilities, etc.)

(5) Income before taxes

(6) Net income

Cost of goods sold includes the direct costs that go into producing your product. The percentage in the box next to this category is the complement of your gross profit margin. In other words, if your cost of goods sold percentage is 69 percent, then your gross profit margin is 31 percent.

Sales and marketing expenses include what it costs you to market and sell your product. In some cases, it costs more than the price of the product to sell it, and only in repeat business is there a reasonable profit margin. It is important to know so that you can price accordingly.

Overhead expenses include all other items such as personnel not in other categories, facilities costs and administrative items such as office supplies, etc.

The *net income* at the bottom of the page should be a budget item, just like the rest of your expenses. I'm not satisfied unless this number is at least 15 percent. Note this will vary by your industry and the economy in general.

To obtain the current year projection (the shaded column), enter the total number from each budget notebook page you filled out for each category. For sales, enter the projection for this year and the actual for last year from the Dollar Sales Projections by Month worksheet (shaded box on bottom right for both years). For other categories, enter the projection number from each budget notebook page and the actual numbers from last year that you added to each budget notebook page.

Calculate the percentage of your total sales that each category makes up by dividing the total number at the bottom of each box by the total sales box at the top. Except for sales, you should have percentages for each of the items listed above.

The last column requires that you determine whether your costs are fixed or variable. Variable costs are those costs that are directly impacted by sales. These costs are expected to change, more or less, in proportion to the change in sales. An example: sales commissions. Fixed costs are all those that are not variable. They don't change as the level of sales increases or decreases. An example: rent.

Some costs may have both a variable piece and a fixed piece. For example, utilities go up as equipment is used more to meet production demands; however, utilities are relatively fixed for most of the office. For purposes of this analysis, expenses that could fall under either category should be classified as fixed.

Total Company Projections

Notebook Item	Current Year Projection	% of sales	Actual Last year	% of sales	Fixed (F) or Variable (V)?
Sales					
Cost of Goods Sold					
Beginning inventory					
Materials purchased					
Salaries & wages					
Production supplies					
Temporary help					
Shipping supplies					
Mailing & shipping					
Less ending inventory					
Total cost of goods sold					
Gross Profit					
Sales & Marketing Expenses					
Salaries					
Sales commissions					
Direct mail					
Advertising					
Publicity					
Consulting					
Other sales & marketing expense					
Total sales & marketing expense					
Overhead Expenses					
Personnel					
Salaries					
Bonuses					
Payroll taxes					
Group life & health insurance					
Workers' comp. insurance					
Employee benefit plans					
Officers' salaries					
Employment expense					
Training					
Temporary help					
Total personnel					
Facilities					
Rents					
Property tax					
Repairs & maintenance					
Utilities					
Property & liability insurance					
Total facilities					
Administration					
Accounting services					
Automobiles					
Bank charges					
Computer supplies					
Contributions					
Depreciation & amortization					
Dues & subscriptions					
Legal services					

Licenses					
Miscellaneous					
Office supplies					
Other professional services					
Retirement plans					
Telephone					
Travel					
Total administration					
Total Overhead Expenses					
Income (Before Taxes)					
Income Taxes					
Net Income					

☐ Are you satisfied with the dollar number and the percentage at the bottom of the page?

☐ Are these numbers higher or lower than last year?

☐ Compare these percentages with industry norms (see resources section in the appendix for sources). Are you higher or lower than others in your industry?

☐ Are category totals as a percentage of sales higher or lower than you would expect?

☐ Have you questioned numbers that seem wrong to you? Do you have back-up calculations or information for all the numbers?

Breakeven Analysis

This worksheet determines the sales level at which the company neither makes a profit nor suffers a loss.

Breakeven analysis can help identify problems and avoid or lessen losses by acting proactively rather than reactively. Obviously, the sooner you recognize that the company is operating at less than breakeven operations, the sooner you can begin to cut fixed costs and take other measures to restore profitability.

Some companies use breakeven analysis in order to evaluate their overall profit goal. It is a simple-to-use tool to relate sales to profit. Breakeven analysis is driven by the relationship of costs, volumes and profits.

Breakeven analysis offers a consistent way to test proposed transactions, consider alternatives or make decisions. Most of the information required to determine your breakeven already exists in your annual budget.

Use the previous Total Company Projections worksheet to determine what costs are fixed and what are variable.

On page one, you will determine the variable cost percentage. This can be done in two ways:

1) Divide the total variable costs by projected sales

   variable cost/sales = *variable cost percentage*

2) Using historical financial statements, divide all variable costs by sales to derive each variable cost as a percentage of sales. Then add all of these percentages to obtain a total variable cost percentage.

Example:

Materials: 50 percent

Production: 10 percent

Direct Labor: 10 percent

Sales salaries: 15 percent

Total Variable Cost: 75 percent

The next step (on page two) is to determine the contribution margin ratio. This ratio is calculated by taking the complement of the variable cost percentage, or simply, subtracting the variable cost percentage from 100 percent.

Contribution Margin Ratio = 100 percent minus the variable cost percent

Now you are ready to calculate your sales breakeven level. To do this, divide total fixed costs by the contribution margin ratio.

Sales Breakeven Level = total fixed costs/contribution margin ratio

Breakeven Analysis — Page 1

% of sales (1)

Variable Expenses —
    Materials purchased
    Production supplies
    Shipping supplies
    Mailing & shipping
    Sales commissions
    Total variable cost %   %

Contribution Margin Ratio   %
(100% — total variable cost %)

Fixed Costs —
    Monthly $
    Annual $

Breakeven Sales Level —
(Fixed cost , contribution margin ratio)
    Monthly $
    Annual $

(1) Current year projections worksheet, % sales column, variable expenses only

Breakeven Analysis — Page 2

	Annual*	Monthly**
Fixed Expenses $		
Personnel		
Salaries & wages — cost of sales		
Salaries — administration		
Bonuses		
Payroll taxes		
Group life & health insurance		
Workers' comp. insurance		
Officers' salaries		
Employment expense		
Training		
Temporary labor		
Total personnel costs $		
Sales & Marketing Expenses		
Salaries		
Direct mail		
Advertising		
Publicity		
Consulting		
Other sales & marketing expense		
Total sales & marketing expense $		
Facilities Expenses		
Rents		
Property tax		
Repairs & maintenance		
Utilities		
Property & liability insurance		
Total facilities expenses $		
Administration		
Accounting services		
Automobiles		
Bank charges		
Computer supplies		
Contributions		
Depreciation & amortization		
Dues & subscriptions		
Interest expense		
Legal services		
Licenses		
Miscellaneous		
Office supplies		
Other professional services		
Retirement plans		
Telephone		
Travel		
Total administration expense $		
Total Fixed Expenses $		

*Current year projections column of *Total Company Projections* worksheet
**Current year projections divided by 12

Ask Yourself:

- ☐ If sales begin to decline, at what level will you start to lose money?

- ☐ If you increase fixed costs by $ X, how much additional sales will you need to generate in order to cover these costs?

- ☐ If you lower the variable cost percentage, what impact will it have on profits?

- ☐ If you want a profit of $ X, what level of sales will you have to achieve?

- ☐ Are there months when your projections are less than breakeven on sales?

Chapter 4: Tracking Profits and Cash

A primary goal of every business is to make enough money to stay in business. Making money can be defined in two ways: making a profit and generating cash. Profitable businesses usually generate cash, but not always. Unprofitable businesses sometimes generate cash, but not often.

Either way, in reviewing your finances, you look at both profits and cash. This chapter takes you through this review by stressing three points:

- The importance of tracking variances from budgeted amounts;

- The importance of cash in running any business; and

- The central role of developing key financial indicators and communicating them to coworkers.

Choosing your key financial indicators depends on the kind of business you run and whether your company is young or mature. As a rule, cash is king for a young company; many start-up owners fear running out of cash more than anything else.

In a mature company, sales and growth may become the main concern. When a company goes public, showing a good return on assets may become paramount.

Flying Blind

The owners of many new businesses fly blind, concentrating on the day-to-day essentials at the expense of reviewing the numbers and planning ahead. But once they start, they discover that the process brings unexpected payoffs in reaching their goals—because it forces them to identify what they want and discover the means by which to get there.

Effective managers develop their own methods for gauging performance, and they define performance in accordance with their short—and long—term goals. They may consider daily revenues, for example, or catalogs mailed, cash balance and payroll.

The small business owner must become intimately involved in the daily dynamics of the business. This familiarity provides a long-term blueprint for keeping the company vital, because the god—or maybe the devil—of implementation is in the details.

Make sure financials are prepared monthly, and preferably by the 10th of the following month, at the latest. Learn which pieces of information in them are relevant to your business and concentrate on those. Don't ignore what the numbers tell you, and above all, believe them; good or bad, the numbers are important.

Don't hesitate to shape the reports you get to suit your ends, either. Accounting departments tend to work by habit, and they sometimes prepare numbers for business managers without giving much thought to making them truly useful. Insist that you get meaningful numbers, laid out as you wish to see them. If you aren't getting them, you have the wrong accounting staff. And the same goes for your CPA.

The Basics: Essential Financial Measurements

Among the basic financial measurements that owners and managers find most important:

Revenue dollars. Your total sales. Is it up or down for the period?

Gross Profit Margin percentage. One of the profit indicators you look at first. This measurement just takes into account the costs directly related to the product manufactured.

Net Income. Always a key indicator of financial performance, it reflects sales and costs, profit and loss—the best places to start any analysis.

Cash position. Especially in the early years of a company's history, liquidity has more importance than any other financial benchmark. But whatever the maturity of your company, it pays to watch how much money you have in the bank at least monthly and maybe weekly.

Accounts payable days and accounts receivable days. Many experts call these leading indicators since they give you a read on what your cash position will be next month. However, accounts receivable are sometimes collected more slowly than payables come due—in which case your cash position becomes tight.

Your management of receivables and payables profoundly affects your cash flow. Poor management here can kill almost any company, no matter what the size, and good management pays big dividends. Just by managing receivables well, even in a small company, you can generate tremendous amounts of cash—in today's economy, the name of the game.

With receivables, a few basic rules apply:

- Develop a good credit-checking system.

- Send your bills out faster, and follow up with phone calls when an account becomes overdue.

- Establish a strict collections schedule and follow it faithfully.

- If your cash flow is strong, you may be willing to give extra time to pay in exchange for additional compensation.

- Keep managers and employees informed when collections become difficult with products they develop, make or sell. They may help with strategies for collecting. They may also know something useful about the customer that will help in collection efforts.

- Don't be afraid to pick up the phone and call the company president.

- Don't wait too long to get attorneys involved if all else fails. A legal letter and some minimal action can often bring about quick payment.

Perhaps the best use of accounts receivable days and payable days as a management tool is to compare the two. Average the time it takes you to pay your bills and the time it takes you to collect. If it takes longer to collect accounts receivable than pay your bills, you're subsidizing customers. If it takes you longer to pay than collect, you're effectively making money from the process.

Inventory. Another way to look at the receivables/payables ratio is as a measure of your financial department's efficiency. Your accounting people must make sure the company pays its bills and collects its receivables on time.

Another cash drain is excess inventory. Without adequate controls over receivables and inventory, it's entirely possible for a company to make a profit and still go out of business.

Whenever and as much as possible, you should integrate inventory management with customer service and delivery programs. The object: to keep as few units on warehouse shelves as you can.

The cost of carrying inventory is expensive. Some manufacturing companies pay 25 to 30 percent of the value of their inventory for the cost of borrowed money, warehouse space, materials handling, staff and transportation expenses related to maintaining it for one financial quarter—three months.

These numbers shock people. Once they realize how expensive inventory can be, they look at it differently. But many owners and managers never make this realization because the cost doesn't show up on any statement. They have to calculate it themselves.

Net worth. This indicator—which, in publicly-traded companies is called shareholders' equity—is simply assets minus liabilities. It includes equity put into the business through the sale of stock or retained earnings. It helps you consider the best ways to allocate equity and assets in order to reach your goals.

Traditional Financial Statements

The traditional financial statement has two components—the income statement and the balance sheet. The income statement shows your sales and expenses, and profit and loss for a given period (usually the month, quarter or year.) The balance sheet shows net worth; it also details such items as inventory, fixed assets, accounts payable and accounts receivable.

Another important financial statement, not always prepared by small companies, is a statement of cash flows. This statement shows you the details of how cash went up or down during the period, and where it went.

Make sure financials are prepared monthly, and preferably by the 10th of the following month, at the latest. Learn what pieces of information are relevant to your business and concentrate on those. Don't ignore what the numbers tell you, and above all, believe them; good or bad, the numbers are important. Don't hesitate to shape the reports you get to suit your ends, either. Accountants tend to work by habit, and they sometimes prepare numbers for business managers without giving much thought to making them truly useful.

In all cases, your financials look backward to show the present—namely your position as of their date of preparation.

On Target From the Start

In many ways, Karen Marchetti considers her company, Rhode Island-based Freight Control Services (FCS), one big experiment. For one thing, her company was the first of its kind in her area, so she had to sell her customers on the services she offered—essentially those of a travel agent for freight shippers. For another, she had no good idea how much demand for her services she would find.

In industry jargon, FCS provides third party logistical services to freight shippers, finding haulers for freight and arranging shipping.

"We started out using my former employer as our first client," Marchetti says. "We had access to their activity history, so we took those numbers, extrapolated figures and theorized how fast the business would grow."

Marchetti started the company in 1991. She had been a consumer of shipping at two companies and saw the opportunity to become a provider of shipping services for companies unwilling or unable to do it for themselves.

In classes offered by the SBA and a local college, she learned how to write a business plan and prepare a financial report. The program also yielded cheap consulting support—two University of Rhode Island undergraduates who helped fine tune her business plan and a graduate student who assisted with sales and marketing research.

Her plan projected sales, costs and profits on a quarterly basis. It covered marketing costs, finances, operations, likely clients, likely suppliers, location and geography. Marchetti found—as is often the case—that she underestimated development costs.

Marchetti and her husband invested $4,000 to buy computers, a fax machine and other equipment to open FCS in a spare room at home. Within a year, Marchetti had rented 300 square feet in a state-subsidized small-business incubator complex, at a subsidized rent. She targeted manufacturers of equipment with special shipping needs—for example, makers of machinery that's easily breakable or decalibrated. Her mission is simple: "We work to enhance the ability of clients to implement cost effective routing programs," Marchetti says.

"Cash flow, all the consultants told me from the beginning, is critical to small business," she adds.

FCS has proven "surprisingly successful" at meeting her projections, Marchetti says—on target from the start and profitable for the first time within two years.

Like the seller of any new product, Marchetti found her focus changing as the company established itself. Customers buy different services than Marchetti thought they would. "Initially we thought customers would want us to do export documents," she says. "They were not as interested in subcontracting that, but they did want us to make transportation arrangements."

In arranging freight for customers, Marchetti developed proprietary software that does much of the work. Since her business is so much like a new product itself, putting together the software seemed a logical progression. In fact, she developed an entire business plan for the new product, just like the one she made for FCS.

And once her company got going, Marchetti took a course in using benchmarks and financial ratios to measure a company's development. This allows her, she says, to "find out where you are in relation to other companies in your fields"—vital knowledge when you bring out something entirely new.

Cash Flow Is Critical

Many small business owners don't think about all the strategies and tools available to them when they run into cash flow problems. Instead, they react by trying to boost sales. They chase revenue, and cost be damned. In so doing, they overextend themselves seeking new business and fail to serve their best customers. This can harm cash flow—the last thing a company needs if liquidity is already a problem.

There are several strategies to maximize cash flow, chief among them controling expenses. Many business owners see expense controls as a sign of trouble, but they aren't. The *absence* of cost controls is a sign of trouble.

"If you don't have cash flow, you can actually grow out of business," says Ball State University professor Donald Kuratko. "If money isn't being collected, it can cause a cash crunch. Even though sales might be up and customers are happy with your product, none of that matters if all your profits are on credit."

If you find your business short of cash, look to your balance sheet and study receivables and inventory—common drains on cash flow.

Key Indicators

Implicit in this discussion is the fact that your concentration on the financials may blind you to opportunity. Budgets set cost targets, leading some managers to spend their time controling how much the operation spends and ignoring how much it earns—or might. They monitor money going out and forget about trends, the big picture, the business underlying the profit and loss statement, which shows results. Worse, they ignore the balance sheet, which shows your financial position.

This single-mindedness is a cost for a business. It turns an organization inward, values rules above initiative and leads managers to query trivial variances while they ignore harder-to-identify, company-wide problems or opportunities. Financial measurements must always be balanced against measures of operations, product development and marketing.

One way to counteract this is developing specific key indicators for your business. A key indicator answers the questions: How well are we really doing? If you were managing the business in crisis mode, and you had to focus only on the essentials, what would you need to know? What numbers or other data would you want on your desk every morning?

In theory, these key indicators measure those items you identified as key success factors in Chapter 2. It is worth spending significant time identifying your business's true key indicators and making sure you have that data consistently available to you.

Follow What Matters

There's nothing like a brush with disaster to show you what matters and what doesn't, as the Wisconsin-based Carson Pirie Scott department store chain learned during a bankruptcy reorganization in 1991. The exercise taught management to improve performance by paying close attention to the company's real-time financial position—key in retailing with its turnover and stiff competition.

Michael MacDonald, chief financial officer, tracks sales and cash position on a monthly—even a weekly—basis.

"You really have to manage a business on a detailed basis and on a frequent basis," MacDonald says. "You don't just look at it now and again. You have to look at it all the time—every day."

The company used a five-inch-thick business plan to chart its way out of bankruptcy. Its creditors insisted that the retailer remain wary of variances from budget. The business plan, MacDonald says, became the company's road map away from disaster.

"There's an axiom in retail that says retail is detail," MacDonald says. "You need to track sales on hand on a very detailed basis. We have pretty sophisticated methods to check what sizes and colors are selling."

For key indicators, managers chart sales per square foot, comparable-store sales growth (to show market share) and operating profit as a percentage of sales and earnings.

Cash and inventory "require continuous fine tuning and monitoring," MacDonald says. The challenge is to make sure that the shortage of cash doesn't choke off the flow of in-demand products.

He describes the goal of his financial scorekeeping bluntly, "The main purpose of a business is to maximize shareholder or investor value." But he watches a number of indicators to achieve that end, all tied to what the company calls the three keys to successful retailing: effective merchandising, giving the customer a positive shopping experience and marketing.

The attention to detail paid off. Within two years, Carson Pirie Scott had earnings of about $33 million on sales of $1.15 billion. Not stellar numbers, but on target with management's goals for averting disaster. By 1998 it had become an acquisition target and its 55 stores became part of Saks, Inc.

Numbers Lag Performance

One key to the success of the Carson Pirie Scott effort was its ability to limit an important shortcoming in financial analysis—the fact that the numbers lag actual performance. Carson Pirie Scott knew that if it tracked expenses, for example, only at the end of each quarter, it would do so too late to make a difference; if you don't look at the money you spend until after you spend it, you look too late.

The financials also can't answer qualitative questions such as those that go into the formulation of your company's vision statement. And you may well find that your financial statement and balance sheet don't address other matters of concern to you. If so, you may need to analyze such items as your return on invested capital, or quality, market share and customer satisfaction.

Ratios and Benchmarking

It is most important, of course, to know how your business is accomplishing the goals you set for it. You can calculate certain ratios that look at both your income statement and your balance sheet and give you an indication of your financial health over time. However, you will also want to compare yourself against your competitors and the industry standards. For many industries, it is possible to compare your ratios to the industry standard and get a sense of how competitive you are as a business. You will certainly want to strive to be in the top half, or better yet, the top quarter.

Sharing Financial Information with Employees

While I certainly advocate sharing financial and other key indicator data with employees, I don't think it makes sense to give them financial statements. Financial statements are documents meant for investors and accountants. They are made a point in time. What employees need are data relevant to their jobs and that data trended to see if improvements are being made.

Find those numbers that will initiate clear action, prepare and present a short written analysis of those numbers. It is vital that each employee see a connection between not only his job, but each individual action and your financials. Virtually every action in business has a financial impact.

Scrupulous Monitoring

Unity Forest Products, Inc., a California-based lumber company, thrives by scrupulously monitoring its cash flow and related items such as inventory, accounts receivable and accounts payable. In a volatile business, it combines efficiency, knowledge of its customers' needs and close attention to financial detail to succeed. Despite that volatility and the plight of the lumber industry in general, the company has never had an unprofitable month.

The company makes sure that profit centers stay profitable. Its employees work hard, producing some six million board feet of lumber each month. CEO Enita Nordeck tracks cash flow each day herself.

Unity started out as a bootstrap operation run by a collection of longtime mill workers who didn't fear competing with the industry's big players. Lumber is a heavily-capitalized, low margin business, and bootstrappers don't usually have the money to get in the game.

Nordeck and her crew needed $1 million to get started. In 1987, when starting out, the management team had only $350,000 in cash. For a short time, Unity bought lumber from sawmills, subcontracted out the resawing, then sold the wood wholesale to lumberyards.

Nordeck had refined a just-in-time inventory management concept into a five-year business plan that depended on weekly cash flow projections—unusual for any startup, let alone one in a volatile commodity business. Unity claimed it could turn inventory over every 10 days; the industry average was 58. The company also claimed it could collect accounts receivable in 10 days; the industry average was 27.

Management looked everywhere for cash to build a new mill but had trouble persuading lenders to back its plan, which lenders considered so aggressive that they doubted its projections. Wells Fargo approved a $150,000 credit line that Unity never touched. Finally, the bank lent Unity the cash to get started.

Nordeck offers her customers a 1 percent discount if they pay within 10 days. In turn, it gets a 2 percent discount from suppliers if Unity pays within 10 days. Competitors see that Unity has figured out that the most significant expense in the lumber industry is carrying a lot of inventory.

Unity also keeps close track of receivables. At one point, a customer who owed the company $40,000 was about to declare bankruptcy. Unity managers drove several company trucks to the customer's plant and repossessed the lumber before sheriff's deputies could arrive to lock up the facility.

The Bottom Line

Many owners and managers are experts at product costs but not with everyday, nonspecific business costs. You can hire consultants or professional staff to study your costs of labor, capital and the rest, but you still need a basic approach to these issues. And you have to know how to judge the results of their work.

Financial realities sometimes conflict with your vision and mission statements. When this happens, you may have to acknowledge the limits of quantitative analysis. Look to your business plan and vision and mission statements for guidance in making cost analysis.

To complete the exercises and worksheets in this section, you'll need:

- Your income statement and balance sheet;
- A list of your accounts payable; and
- A list of your accounts receivable.

You may need to gather other data as well. The worksheets and formulas on the following pages that flow from this information will help you:

- Compare projections to actual sales and expenses through your fiscal year;
- Analyze cash flow;
- Calculate and analyze various financial ratios; and
- Determine key financial indicators and other information critical to owners, managers and employees.

Put together, the worksheets and exercises provide you with useful financial tools, and the framework for a monthly reporting package that will allow you to monitor your company's performance from many different perspectives and take some appropriate actions.

Ask Yourself:

- ☐ Do you have good cash management?
- ☐ Do you have timely and accurate financial data to review?
- ☐ Does the data you have help you make decisions? Do you need more? Do you look at all the data you receive each month?
- ☐ Is your company performing well compared to industry standards?
- ☐ Do you meet with employees at least once a month to review variances and trends?

Year at a Glance Income Statement

The income statement tells you how well your company has done over a period of time. It shows both your revenue and your expenses, and arrives at a net income number at the bottom of the page.

Financial reports done by your accountants are useful comparing this year to last year, but they don't tell you whether there is a big variation from projection and which month the variation may have occurred. If there is a large variation in one month, the year to date numbers are off the rest of the year after that point.

The worksheet synthesizes many important numbers into one form—on one page. It offers a visual way to look at everything at once, which helps you think about business activities over the course of a whole year. Large variances become quickly apparent.

Using this worksheet, I find myself better prepared to ask pointed questions about budget items. I can compare them to other items, even other budget variances.

Of course, some of these items may result from miscoding and similar technical problems, rather than expenses being much different than expected. But even glitches become easier to detect when the numbers run alongside one another.

Enter your actual sales and expense numbers each month throughout the year. Calculate the monthly average column by taking the number of months into the year you are, and dividing by that number.

This tells you if your monthly average is over your original budget and whether your current month is above or below average.

Ask Yourself:

☐ Are your expenses what you expected, or are there large variations?

☐ Does each month look comparable, or are there large differences month to month?

☐ Do particular items seem out of line with the others in the report?

☐ Can you see trends that run across your business functions?

☐ Are there certain budget items that play well compared against one another? What do those comparisons mean about your business functions?

Go to worksheets on the following pages ➔

Year At A Glance Income Statement — Page 1-2

	Jan.	Feb.	March	April	May
Sales					
Cost of Goods Sold					
Beginning inventory					
Materials purchased					
Salaries & wages					
Production supplies					
Temporary help					
Shipping supplies					
Mailing & shipping					
Less ending inventory					
Total cost of goods sold					
Gross Profit					
Sales & Marketing Expenses					
Salaries					
Sales commissions					
Direct mail					
Advertising					
Publicity					
Consulting					
Other sales & marketing expense					
Total sales & marketing expense					
Overhead Expenses					
Personnel					
Salaries					
Bonuses					
Payroll taxes					
Group life & health insurance					
Workers' comp. insurance					
Employee benefit plans					
Officers' salaries					
Employment expense					
Training					
Temporary help					
Total personnel					

June	July	Aug	Sept.	Oct.	Nov.	Dec.	Total	Mo. Avg.

Year At A Glance Income Statement — Page 3-4

	Jan.	Feb.	March	April	May	June
Facilities						
Rents						
Property tax						
Repairs & maintenance						
Utilities						
Property & liability insurance						
Total facilities						
Administration						
Accounting services						
Automobiles						
Bank charges						
Computer supplies						
Contributions						
Depreciation & amortization						
Dues & subscriptions						
Legal services						
Licenses						
Miscellaneous						
Office supplies						
Other professional services						
Retirement plans						
Telephone						
Travel						
Total administration						
Total Overhead Expenses						
Income (Before Taxes)						
Income Taxes						
Net Income						

July	Aug.	Sept.	Oct.	Nov.	Dec.	Total

July	Aug.	Sept.	Oct.	Nov.	Dec.	Total

July	Aug.	Sept.	Oct.	Nov.	Dec.	Total

July	Aug.	Sept.	Oct.	Nov.	Dec.	Total

July	Aug.	Sept.	Oct.	Nov.	Dec.	Total

Year at a Glance Balance Sheet

This worksheet illustrates items in your balance sheet in a format for easy analysis, month to month. It's a statement of what the company owns at a fixed point in time. It remains important to look at changes occurring from month to month because there is a direct relationship between changes in your balance sheet and your cash flow.

The Year at a Glance Balance Sheet allows you to track balance sheet accounts for trends. It also allows you a measurement system to track goals: you may have to decrease inventory or decrease accounts receivable (both of which would increase your cash).

The most important accounts to focus on are cash, accounts receivable, inventory, fixed assets and accounts payable. More obscure accounts like Other Assets generally don't change much month to month, so you don't need to focus on them. This format allows you to see important changes if they occur.

Most smaller and more aggressive owners and managers pay close attention to accounts receivable and payable on this worksheet. They affect cash flow in mercilessly direct ways:

- If accounts receivable go up—your cash goes down
- If inventory goes down—your cash goes up
- If accounts payable goes down—your cash goes down
- If fixed assets go up—your cash goes down.

Find the items below from your monthly balance sheet and enter each month on the worksheet. You will usually find these items on the balance sheet divided by current (usually one year or less) or long term.

Chapter 4: Tracking Profits and Cash

ASSETS

Current Assets

Cash

Accounts Receivable—money owed to you by your customers

Inventory—your product waiting to be sold, either at your location or at a store

Prepaid Expenses—items such as insurance or taxes (example: an insurance premium is paid up front for a whole year; this entry spreads it out over the policy period)

Other Current Assets—miscellaneous items like rent deposits

Fixed Assets—real property, equipment and leasehold improvements

Accumulated Depreciation

Net Fixed Assets

Intangible Assets—good will, intellectual property—rights to something, trademarks, patents

LIABILITIES

Current Liabilities—an amount you owe to someone else, generally to be paid within one year

Notes Payable

Accounts Payable

Accrued Liabilities

Long Term Debt

EQUITY

Retained Earnings—the amount of net income the company has earned and kept since the first day of the business, less dividends to shareholders

Year At A Glance Balance Sheet

	Jan.	Feb.	March	April
ASSETS				
Cash				
Accounts Receivable				
Inventory				
Prepaid Expenses				
Other Current Assets				
Total Current Assets				
Fixed Assets				
Accumulated Depreciation				
Net Fixed Assets				
Intangible Assets				
Other Assets				
TOTAL ASSETS				
LIABILITIES				
Current Portion Long-Term Debt				
Notes Payable				
Accounts Payable				
Accrued Liabilities				
Other Current Liabilities				
Total Current Liabilities				
Long Term Debt				
Other Liabilities				
Total Liabilities				
EQUITY				
Common Stock				
Paid in Capital				
Retained Earnings				
TOTAL EQUITY AND LIABILITIES				

May	June	July	Aug.	Sept.	Oct.	Nov.	Dec.

Ask Yourself:

☐ Are your accounts receivable and accounts payable accounts up or down over the period?

☐ Are there sharp variations during certain peak periods or seasons?

☐ Is your cash consistently at a comfortable level for operating the business?

☐ What is the current trend in inventory levels?

☐ Has your company acquired fixed assets in accordance with capital budgets?

Year At a Glance Financial Analysis

This exercise pulls together useful information from both the balance sheet and income statement and calculates some ratios to give you an idea of the financial health of the company and how it changes month to month.

The ratios included here are generally computed for whole industries. It is useful to compare your numbers to your industry.

The Balance Sheet items are asset management related and tell you how well you are doing increasing the value of what you own. The Income Statement items are related to profitability and tell you how well you are doing in that area.

This worksheet, as with the other year at a glance worksheets, gives you a quick indication of how things are changing over time. The problem with financial statements is that you can't tell whether things have gotten better or worse this month. These will let you know immediately if there is a sudden downturn or a trend in that direction so that you can take corrective action.

Find the numbers for the first four categories from your income statement and enter them for the appropriate month. Also enter the number of people you currently employ. Divide sales by number of employees to get the number for the last category under the Income Statement, sales per employee.

Enter the numbers for the first three entries under Balance Sheet. The remainder of the categories are calculated as follows:

Sales. Take this item from your Income Statement.

Gross Profit Margin. This ratio is Sales minus Cost of Goods Sold divided by Sales.

Pre-tax profit. Take this item from your Income Statement.

Cumulative Net Income. An aggregate of the monthly income figures listed for the year to date, this tells you how close you are to your projections for the year.

Number of Employees. Take this item from your Payroll Projection worksheets.

Sales per Employee. This number divides your sales figure by the number of people the company employs to generate that figure. This is a popular tool for determining a company's efficiency—though standards change dramatically by industry.

Total Current Assets. Take this item from your Balance Sheet.

Total Current Liabilities. Take this item from your Balance Sheet.

Working Capital. The amount by which Current Assets exceed Current Liabilities.

Current Ratio. A basic test of solvency, you obtain this number by dividing the current assets of your company by current liabilities.

Sales to Assets. A measure of how aggressively the business pursues sales, this figure (Total Current Assets divided by Sales) helps analysts determine how much unrealized sales potential a company might have.

Year At A Glance Financial Analysis

		Jan.	Feb.	March	April
	Income Statement				
1.	Sales				
2.	Gross Profit Margin				
3.	Pre Tax Profit				
4.	Cumulative Net Income				
5.	Number of Employees				
6.	Sales Per Employee				
	Balance Sheet				
7.	Total Current Assets				
8.	Total Current Liabilities				
9.	Working Capital				
10.	Current Ratio				
11.	Sales to Assets				
12.	Return on Assets				
13.	Debt to Equity				
14.	Accounts Receivable Days				
15.	Accounts Payable Days				
16.	Inventory Turnover (annually)				
17.	Inventory Turn Days				

May	June	July	Aug.	Sept.	Oct.	Nov.	Dec.

Return on Assets. This figure (Pre Tax Profit divided by Total Assets) compares profit with the amount of assets used to earn that profit. Acceptable figures vary from industry to industry.

Debt to Equity. This figure (Total Liabilities divided by Net Worth or Shareholders' Equity) relates the company's debt to the strength of the equity in the company by owners or stockholders.

Accounts Receivable Days. First, divide Sales by Accounts Receivable to obtain accounts receivable turnover. Then, divide 365 by the turnover figure. The result (also called Collection Period Ratio) indicates how many days people are taking to pay you.

Accounts Payable Days. First, divide your Cost of Goods Sold by Accounts Payable to obtain accounts payable turnover. Then, divide 365 by the turnover figure. The result indicates how many days you're taking to pay your bills. It also tells analysts about your company's liquidity.

Inventory Turnover (annually). This figure (Cost of Goods Sold divided by the Inventory item from your Balance Sheet) provides an indicator of how many times a year your company turns over its entire inventory.

Inventory Turn Days. Obtained by dividing 365 by the annual Inventory Turnover figure, this figure gives you a time period to compare directly with the Accounts Receivable and Payable numbers listed above.

Clearly, this worksheet will be one of the most valuable when you're dealing with potential lenders or investors. In this context, financial analysts sometimes ask for ratios not included on this worksheet. Some of the most important include:

Current liabilities/inventory. Obtained by dividing current liabilities by the value of current inventory, this figure tells managers how much the company relies on funds yet to be obtained from unsold inventories to meet its debt obligations.

Net sales/working capital. By measuring the number of times working capital turns over annually in relation to net sales, this ratio provides information about whether the business relies too heavily on credit to maintain its sales effort.

Return on Investment. This figure prorates net profit by an individual investment vehicle's percentage of a company's total capitalization. It tells investors how soon they will recoup their money; it tells managers what form investments should take (limited partnerships, preferred or common stock, etc.).

Current liabilities/net worth. Considered by some lenders the most important test of a company's solvency, this figure indicates the amount due creditors within a year as a percentage of the investment in the business by owners or stockholders.

Ask Yourself:

- ☐ Which numbers are trended in a positive direction, and which in a negative direction? Are your ratios in line with industry averages?

- ☐ Which ratios concern you most? Are these issues that require immediate solutions (for example: the current ratio) or long-term solutions (for example: sales per employee)?

- ☐ Is the overall financial condition of the company getting better or worse?

- ☐ Can unusual or negative trends be explained satisfactorily?

- ☐ Are there other ratios that are particularly important to your business that should be included?

Budget Variance Report

This worksheet gives an easy way to compare your actual numbers each month to your budget numbers, both for that month and the year to date (cumulative for the whole year).

Budget Variance Report — Page 1-2

	Month To Date		
Plan $	Actual $	$ Variance	% Variance

Sales

Cost of Goods Sold

Beginning inventory			
Materials purchased			
Salaries & wages			
Production supplies			
Temporary help			
Shipping supplies			
Mailing & shipping			
Less ending inventory			
Total cost of goods sold			

Gross Profit

Sales & Marketing Expenses

Salaries			
Sales commissions			
Direct mail			
Advertising			
Publicity			
Consulting			
Other sales & marketing expense			
Total sales & marketing expense			

Overhead Expenses

Personnel

Salaries			
Bonuses			
Payroll taxes			
Group life & health insurance			
Workers comp. insurance			
Employee benefit plans			
Officers' salaries			
Employment expense			
Training			
Temporary help			
Total personnel			

Year To Date			
Plan $	Actual $	$ Variance	% Variance

Budget Variance Report — Page 3-4

	Month To Date		
Plan $	Actual $	$ Variance	% Variance

Facilities
Rents
Property Tax
Repairs & maintenance
Utilities
Property & liability insurance
Total facilities

Administration
Accounting services
Automobiles
Bank charges
Computer supplies
Contributions
Depreciation & amortization
Dues & subscriptions
Legal services
Licenses
Miscellaneous
Office supplies
Other professional services
Retirement plans
Telephone
Travel
Total administration
Total Overhead Expenses

Income (Before Taxes)

Income Taxes

Net Income

Year To Date			
Plan $	Actual $	$ Variance	% Variance

Business Plans to Game Plans

Managers go through all the effort of making a budget each year, but unless they compare their actual financial picture to what they budgeted, doing the budget remains a meaningless exercise. Budget variance is a wake up call for managers to make mid-course corrections, and to replan for the remainder of the year. With any variance, a manager should investigate what's gone right or wrong, and hold people accountable for their spending.

This worksheet is also very illustrative for employee meetings and board of directors meetings.

Enter your budget numbers for each item for the current month. Then enter the actual numbers that correspond to each category. In the third column, take the difference between the two (actual minus plan), and enter it in the "$ variance" column. For expense items, a negative number means you're under budget and a positive number means you spent more than you expected.

Lastly, calculate the % variance by dividing the $ variance by the plan $. A negative $ variance will result in a negative % variance. Complete the whole exercise again for year-to-date numbers.

Notice that all the reports in this section have the same categories in the same order as the original budget. This makes comparisons between budget and actual much easier.

Ask Yourself:

☐ Are there variances from budget of 10 percent or more (and $500 or more)? What accounts for these?

☐ If these variances are in the Year to Date column, are they also in the current month or did they take place in a prior month?

☐ Are variances in Cost of Goods Sold influencing your gross profit margin?

☐ Are your variances in the areas most companies find difficult to control: sales, marketing and personnel?

☐ If the variance is negative, can you make immediate changes in your operations that will reduce the variance from budget?

☐ If the variance is positive, are you spending enough to support (what is probably) the increase in sales? Do you expect this increase in sales to continue?

Same Month Last Year Variance Report

This exercise allows comparison between individual months this year with the same months last year. This comparison allows for cyclical trends and historical perspective that many managers use as a basis for forecasting.

It's important to compare your current numbers to prior years, especially when you're trying to grow a company. At publicly-traded companies, stockholders always want to see if the company is doing better than last year.

Budgets can be wildly above or below actual performance. Unforeseen factors can change the business a company does in a given time period. Projections—even good ones—are always suspect. Last year's actuals are reality.

For the same month last year, enter your sales and expense numbers. Then use the same numbers from the Budget Variance worksheet to fill in the second column for the current month. Subtract last year from this year, and divide that number by last year to get the percent difference. A positive percentage indicates an increase from last year to this year.

Do the same calculations again with year-to-date numbers.

Ask Yourself:

☐ Is the variance great again? If so, do some investigation into what changed from last year.

☐ Are there variances greater than 10 percent? If so, can you explain them in a way that makes sense?

Same Month Last Year Variance Report — Page 1

	Month to Date			Year to Date		
	Last Year $	This Year $	% Difference	Last Year $	This Year $	% Difference
Sales						
Cost of Goods Sold						
Beginning inventory						
Materials purchased						
Salaries & wages						
Production supplies						
Temporary help						
Shipping supplies						
Mailing & shipping						
Less ending inventory						
Total cost of goods sold						
Gross Profit						
Sales & Marketing Expenses						
Salaries						
Sales commissions						
Direct mail						
Advertising						
Publicity						
Consulting						
Other sales & marketing						
Total sales & marketing						
Overhead Expenses						
Personnel						
Salaries						
Bonuses						
Payroll taxes						
Group life/health ins						
Workers' comp ins						
Empl benefit plans						
Officers' salaries						
Employment exp						
Training						
Temporary help						
Total personnel						

Same Month Last Year Variance Report — Page 2

	Month to Date			Year to Date		
	Last Year $	This Year $	% Difference	Last Year $	This Year $	% Difference
Facilities						
Rents						
Property tax						
Repairs & maintenance						
Utilities						
Property & liability						
Insurance						
Total facilities						
Administration						
Accounting services						
Automobiles						
Bank charges						
Computer supplies						
Contributions						
Depreciation & amortization						
Dues & subscriptions						
Legal services						
Licenses						
Miscellaneous						
Office supplies						
Other professional services						
Retirement plans						
Telephone						
Travel						
Total administration						
Total Overhead Expenses						
Income (Before Taxes)						
Income Taxes						
Net Income						

- ☐ Are your expenses up in any one category more than another?

- ☐ If the variance comes in the Year to Date column, in what month did it begin to occur?

- ☐ Are you prepared for any cyclicality you see with adequate cash?

Top 20 Customers Who Owe Us Money

This worksheet keeps close track of the accounts receivable and helps to set a strategy to collect the money as soon as possible.

It is important to carefully track customers who bought your company's product on credit but haven't paid as they have agreed to within a specific time. The older the bills get, the less likely they will be paid.

It's important for managers to have a plan to get people to pay, and the first step in that is to know who owes money, how long they've owed it and how much they owe. Sometimes the top 20 can account for most of the money owed to a company, if it has several large customers.

Doing something as simple as concentrating on getting paid by these people can have a significant impact on raising a company's cash position.

List the customers who owe you money and rank them from the largest dollar volume to the smallest. Enter the top 10, from largest to smallest on this worksheet.

Across the columns, show the total these customers owe and their balances (that equal this total) in each category of days overdue.

In the comments section, list their likelihood of paying, when you last contacted them, etc.

At the bottom of the worksheet, calculate how much money the top 20 represent compared to your total receivables.

Ask Yourself:

□ What percentage do your top 20 receivables represent of your accounts receivable?

□ Are any of the customers on the list still buying on credit?

□ Do you have limits as to how much credit you will allow?

□ Are there trends that connect the type of customer and the amount of money owed?

□ Are there trends in the business or industry sector that connect the type of customer and the amount owed?

□ Are there economic factors that explain trends in receivables?

Go to worksheet on the following page   →

Top 20 Customers Who Owe Us Money

(Accounts Receivable Ranked by $ Volume)

Name	Customer Account #	Total Dollar Amount Owed
1.		
2.		
3.		
4.		
5.		
6.		
7.		
8.		
9.		
10.		
11.		
12.		
13.		
14.		
15.		
16.		
17.		
18.		
19.		
20.		

Total receivables (from financial statement)

Date _____

Past Due Balances				Comments
30	60	90	120+	
Totals				

$$\frac{\text{TOP 20 \$}}{\text{TOTAL REC.}} \quad \boxed{} \quad \%$$

Analysis of Cash Position

This worksheet shows where money went besides paying for the expenses itemized in the Income Statement. A company made money but doesn't have cash to show for it. Why? Where did the cash go and how much was used up by the operations and how much was consumed by other things?

It will analyze where the company's cash comes from—and goes.

This worksheet is a variation of the accountant's Statement of Changes in Cash, which is a required part of a publicly-traded company's financial reporting.

There are three areas of cash use shown in this worksheet:

(1) Cash used for operations—Cash flows from operating activities are generally the cash impact of changes in working capital accounts and from the basic operations of the company. Examples of increases to cash would include net income, collection of accounts receivables, decreases in inventory and depreciation. Examples of decreases to cash would include a net loss, increases in accounts receivable balances, increases in inventory and payments of accounts payable.

(2) Cash used for investing activities (buying fixed assets, making acquisitions).

(3) Cash used for financing activities (repayment of bank debt, long-term leases).

Enter in the numbers called for both for the current month and year to date from your income statement (first line only) and from your balance sheet (remainder of the worksheet). Total the numbers in the shaded boxes to find your net increase or decrease in cash for the period.

This is a complex worksheet. You may wish to get assistance from your CPA, especially if you have sales and fixed assets changes during the period.

Analysis of Cash Position

	Current Month	YTD
Operating Activities:		
Net Income/(Loss)		
Adjustments to Reconcile Net Income/Loss to Cash		
Depreciation & Amortization		
Changes in Assets & Liabilities:		
(Increase) Decrease in Accounts Receivable		
(Increase) Decrease in Inventory		
(Increase) Decrease in Prepaid Expenses		
(Increase) Decrease in Other Current Assets		
Increase (Decrease) in Accounts Payable		
Increase (Decrease) in Current Portion Long-Term Debt		
Increase (Decrease) in Accrued Liabilities		
Total Adjustments		
Net Cash Provided By (Used For) Operating Activities		

	Current Month	YTD
Investing Activities:		
Additions to Fixed Assets		
(Increase) Decrease in Other Assets		
Other		
Net Cash Provided By (Used For) Investing Activities		

	Current Month	YTD
Financing Activities:		
Line of Credit Borrowings (repayments)		
Principle Payments on Long-Term Debt		
Net Cash From (Used For) Financing Activities		

	Current Month	YTD
Net Increase (Decrease) In Cash For Period		

	Current Month	YTD
Cash @ Beginning of Period		

	Current Month	YTD
Cash @ End of Period		

Ask Yourself:

☐ Was there a net increase or decrease to your cash for the period? For the year?

☐ Was the change from operational factors, investing factors or financing factors?

☐ Are there changes you can make to positively influence your cash position?

☐ Is the company generating positive cash flow from operations?

☐ If the company is losing money, how is that loss being financed? With new equity? With payables?

Key Financial Indicators

This worksheet provides a one-page comparison of all of the key financial numbers comparing two years past to the current year.

Used well, it will give managers a broad view, over three years, of trends in their business that relate to cash.

I use this sheet at Board meetings and to give to employees to illustrate, in simple terms, how the company is doing. It is a communications tool for displaying analysis I've done in other worksheets and exercises.

Keep a running total on all of your major financial numbers—cash, revenue, expenses and income—and enter the current month when available.

Record your accounts receivable and accounts payable days, as well as your total accounts receivable.

Ask Yourself:

☐ Are the long-term trends (taking up the entire three years) what you want them to be?

☐ Have expense increases outpaced revenue increases?

Key Financial Indicators

CASH

		Jan.	Feb.	March	April	May	June	July	Aug.	Sept.	Oct.	Nov.	Dec.
This year	Proj												
	Act												
Last year	Act												
Two years ago	Act												

Revenue

	Jan.	Feb.	March	April	May	June	July	Aug.	Sept.	Oct.	Nov.	Dec.
This year												
Last year												
Two years ago												

Expenses

		Jan.	Feb.	March	April	May	June	July	Aug.	Sept.	Oct.	Nov.	Dec.
This year	Proj												
	Act												
Last year	Act												
Two years ago	Act												

Income Month To Date & Year To Date

		Jan. MTD	YTD	Feb. MTD	YTD	March MTD	YTD	April MTD	YTD	May MTD	YTD	June MTD	YTD
This year	Proj												
	Act												
Last year	Act												
Two years ago	Act												

		July MTD	YTD	Aug. MTD	YTD	Sept. MTD	YTD	Oct. MTD	YTD	Nov. MTD	YTD	Dec. MTD	YTD
This year	Proj												
	Act												
Last year	Act												
Two years ago	Act												

Accounts Receivable Days

	Jan.	Feb.	March	April	May	June	July	Aug.	Sept.	Oct.	Nov.	Dec.
This year												
Last year												
Two years ago												

Accounts Payable Days

	Jan.	Feb.	March	April	May	June	July	Aug.	Sept.	Oct.	Nov.	Dec.
This year												
Last year												
Two years ago												

Accounts Receivable

	Jan.	Feb.	March	April	May	June	July	Aug.	Sept.	Oct.	Nov.	Dec.
CURRENT												
30+												
60+												
90+												
120+												
TOTAL												

☐ Are accounts receivable days and accounts payable days increasing or decreasing?

☐ Are overdue accounts receivable increasing or decreasing?

☐ Does this worksheet accurately display the financial strengths and weaknesses that your company has?

Financial Report to Employees

This worksheet—also a communications tool—provides a simple way to keep employees informed about those key indicators upon which they can have an impact and help keep the company financially healthy.

Consider sending this worksheet and its attachments to all employees every month. In addition, have a monthly meeting to go over these numbers and answer questions about what they mean, and how they relate to each job done in the company.

Enter the numbers from the Key Financial Indicators worksheet for the current month as well as a running total for the year to date.

Provide a simple analysis at the bottom of the page by determining which of your key items is up or down and translating the importance of these items for your employees.

Attach the important financial worksheets developed in this section.

Ask Yourself:

☐ Are you on target for where you expected to be at this point in the year?

☐ Are there things employees can do to help your company reach its financial goals and projections?

☐ Do employees understand the numbers and concepts presented in this worksheet? If not, how long will it take to teach them the things they need to know?

TO: All Employees

Financial Report to Employees
for _____
(month/year)

	Current Month	Prior Month	Two Months Ago	YTD
Sales				
Expenses: Cost of Goods Sold				
Gross Profit Margin				
Sales Expenses				
Administration				
Total Expense				
Income (sales minus expenses)				
Cash				
Inventory $:				
A/R Days:				
A/P Days:				
Inventory Turndays:				

Attachments:

1. <u>Year at a Glance Income Statement</u>

   Sales were (above/below) projections by _____%.

   Expenses were (over/under) budget by _____%. Especially over budget
   were the following items:

2. <u>Key Financial Indicators</u>

   Profits were (above/below) projections by _____%.

3. <u>Analysis of Cash Position</u>

   Our cash was (under/over) projections by _____%.

Comments:

Business Plans to Game Plans

- ☐ Are you celebrating good news and acknowledging the effect of the hard work of particular employees?

- ☐ Do you ask the employees responsible for the changes you see to provide the explanation to the rest of the employees?

CHAPTER 5:

MARKETING AND PRODUCT DEVELOPMENT

No business factor irritates, perplexes and challenges owners and managers more than marketing—perhaps because the term covers so many activities and disciplines. In many companies it includes sales, customer research and new product development.

This confusion leads some managers away from giving marketing the attention it deserves. Successful companies boast that they are market responsive or market driven, but in truth, in a world that depends on information, all companies must be market responsive. Your customers don't buy your products or those of your competitors for mysterious reasons, and whether you make hardware for cars, disk drives for computers or movies for Hollywood, you must know your customers—who they are and what they want. You must notice when their wants and needs change.

Marketing Overview

Delivering better products faster and more efficiently to your customers requires lots of information. Marketing—in its broadest definition—*is* that information. It's a means of figuring out what works and what doesn't work for your business.

This chapter takes you through this process by:

- Considering your industry's potential and your competitors;
- Reviewing marketing activities to date; and
- Looking at the development of new products.

Business Plans to Game Plans

The details of the marketing plan will vary greatly depending on the business. In publishing, for example, marketing entails huge expenses for advertising, publicity and distribution because selling books or data relies on thousands of small and sometimes impulsive transactions. Marketing in the defense industry, on the other hand, entails meeting new customers face-to-face and networking on Capitol Hill and in the Pentagon. This is because defense contracting relies on a few huge and thoroughly considered transactions.

First, you must consider how large or small your market is, and who are the other players in that market.

You learn a lot from the people in the marketplace who love your products and even more from those who don't. This means taking a hard look at your successes and your failures. It also means researching how well others are doing, and analyzing that data to see what will be useful in your marketing efforts.

Whoever and wherever they are, your customers can get just about anything they want at any time they want it. They can get the things or services they want from you or from someone else, and usually on terms close to their own. Consumers have grown accustomed to getting better products faster and with high-quality service. In fact, products are generally sold on one or more of three criteria—quality, value (a more useful concept than cost) and service. The challenge to your marketing efforts is to determine what combination of these basics works most effectively for the product you make.

Marketing well may take more planning than any other area of your business; most businesses have a specifically developed marketing plan. They include not only an assessment of the world at large, but also what activities you will undertake to impact that world and reach your customers. Your customers perception is critical; your message to them about your product must be clear, striking and allow them to immediately see the benefit in buying your product.

How will you get that message out to them? What media will you use? How will you distribute your product? These are all questions to be answered in your marketing plan.

And out of good marketing research comes ideas for new product development. What else do your customers expect you to provide them? What are the potential risks and what other opportunities will you have to forego in order to launch a specific new product?

External Forces — Research Your Market

It's easy to pose the questions you want to answer about your market and your competitors—and difficult to answer them. Managers must usually do more with less when looking outside the organization for factors influencing sales. Among the most important of these questions:

- What is your position in your industry?

- What are the sales and profit trends in your sector?

- What are the product trends? What's hot? What's cold?

- How do you expect your industry to change in the next year? In the next five years?

- What are the strengths and weaknesses of your competitors' products? Of their management teams?

- How do they mix quality, value and service?

- Can you bring new products to market more quickly than your competitors?

Begin your market research by asking everyone in your company to write down everything they know about your competition and its products. From this, expect to pull a variety of impressions; your sales staff will probably have a different perspective than your technical people.

Order your competitors' products, call their salespeople, visit them at trade shows and look at their Web sites. Make a point of collecting and discussing this data at least annually. The object is to build a universe where you can place and define your product and how your customers perceive you. You want to understand your competition so you can differentiate your product.

Knowing your marketplace has a direct impact on what you do. A management consultant from the Midwest tells the story of an inventor with little marketing experience who invented a new toy—a great product combining mechanical simplicity with endless variations in outcome. The excited inventor couldn't wait to bring his product to market.

The problem: he wasn't sure what—or where—that market existed.

He needed a partner who knew toy marketing. He found one, but the partner didn't understand the appeal of the inventor's toy. Instead, the marketer came to the deal with a load of preconceived notions about how to sell consumer products that didn't fit the product. The partners failed to get the toy on retail shelves or create word-of-mouth publicity. They sold through mail order catalogues, but the toy didn't take off with consumers.

Several years and one partnership later, the inventor had to start over, taking the time to learn how a tight-knit industry like children's toys works and what one must do to get a product recognized.

Researching Customer Buying Patterns

This is becoming much less difficult with the services available on the World Wide Web. It is possible to collect so much data on customers and their buying patterns that consumer groups have become alarmed and have tried to stop it.

It is important to know what data you need and not get bogged down in just having a lot of data. You need data about customers you have and the ones you have missed, relevant to your particular product or service. That will be plenty to focus on.

Chapter 5: Marketing and Product Development

Marketing Data

A well-coordinated marketing effort helps you diagnose and solve problems related to the external factors that affect your sales—for example, a widespread recession. California-based marketing consultant Molly Thorpe reports that during the recession of the early 1990s, nine out of 10 of her clients focused their marketing efforts on boosting profitability rather than increasing revenues against the economic currents.

According to Thorpe, most companies use marketing information weakly and ineffectively. "Many businesses don't focus on who their real customers are because they are afraid to turn away business," she says. "But it's important to identify who you don't want to sell to, so you don't squander your resources."

To do this, you need good information about your sales and customers. It is important to chart the information about sales and customers through time by week, month, or year; by product type, location, customer type; by marketing method, dollar volume and any other way that fits with your business. This will be the work of the next chapter.

Constructing a matrix—a graphic structure that gives form to disparate pieces of information—allows you to illustrate the information you've collected. This helps you look at the information from a variety of perspectives—upside down and sideways, friendly and antagonistic.

A Solid Plan

Jeffrey Schmidt and Clark Greenlee, who started a successful espresso bar in the Country Club shopping district of Kansas City, shared a clear eye on their market when they started out.

Working as architects in Washington, D.C., they saw running an espresso bar as a good way to put their design skills to practical use. Coffee bars had proliferated in Washington, and Schmidt figured that Kansas City, his home town, might prove a good market for a business relying heavily on atmosphere and inexpensive extravagance.

He and Greenlee first conducted some basic market research. They went to espresso bars whenever they had the chance. They enrolled in small business administration (SBA) classes on starting a business and writing business plans. They contacted officials in Kansas City.

In 1991, Schmidt started scouting locations. He focused on the Country Club Plaza, a shopping and business district south of downtown with good foot traffic—essential for an espresso bar.

He contacted J.C. Nichols Co., a big real estate management firm that runs the Country Club district. Nichols liked the concept and asked to see a business plan.

Their Own Strengths

It took them three months to put a plan together. The plan reflected Schmidt and Greenlee's strengths in architecture. It forecast sales and cash flow and analyzed the Kansas City marketplace and the performance of analogous cafes and restaurants. Schmidt and Greenlee projected that they could do well if they sold 400 cups of espresso a day. That figure seemed in line with comparable shops in comparable markets.

Nichols had seen other pitches from people who wanted to start espresso bars in the Country Club Plaza. It chose Schmidt and Greenlee because they best understood the market for an upscale coffee place.

With the landlord on their side, Schmidt and Greenlee began meeting with bankers in Kansas City. Between them, the partners had $30,000 to invest. United Missouri Bank lent them another $70,000 under a SBA program.

"They had a great business plan; they came in and presented it very well and they seemed sharp and on the ball—qualities we look for in a borrower," said the bank officer who made the loan.

With financing arranged, Schmidt and Greenlee signed a lease with Nichols for a prime spot in the Country Club Plaza. The partners then started a crash course in managing espresso bars; Greenlee worked at a successful outlet back in Washington. They lined up contractors and permits and polished their designs for the store, knowing that the look would play a key role in its success. Throughout, Schmidt and Greenlee showed their knowledge of their customers—young urbanites seeking attractive places to spend time.

Latteland Espresso opened in spring 1993. By the end of the year, it had become one of the most thriving locations in the Country Club Plaza. Sales ran 50 percent ahead of projections and the place already turned a healthy profit.

Marketing Activities

Sales are the best tool for measuring the effectiveness of your marketing activities, but they don't tell you everything you need to know. If sales increase, you're doing something right. But it sometimes takes some digging to find out what. You want to make the best and most effective use of your sales resources, and you need to analyze your numbers so that you know what "best" and "most effective" mean.

This includes looking for the highest margin. Find out what the average gross profit margin is for your industry and market and see whether you expect to outdo or fall below the standard—and whether you can stay in business at that margin.

But immediate profit isn't everything, especially when you undertake a long-term marketing program. Such a program might call for you to cultivate satisfied customers who believe they get their money's worth and will come back a second and third time. This may require you to sacrifice short-term profitability—a good sacrifice if you like your chances over the long term.

There are many ways to reach customers; the key is to know how to reach the customers that will be interested in what you have to offer.

Marketing activities include:

- Advertising
- Direct mail
- Newsletters
- Public relations
- Catalogs
- Telemarketing
- Sales lead generation

Great effort will likely be spent (whatever activity or combination of activities you choose) on telling the customer about your product. Tell your customers how your product will enhance their lives and show them your sympathy for their exact situation.

Also, know what you want to accomplish with a specific marketing activity. Do you want to increase awareness? Draw someone into your location? Have them call your sales office? Buy from your Web site? Order from your catalog? Be sure and give them the most effective way to contact you.

Don't neglect tracking your results meticulously. In the course of our business, we did a lot of direct mail. It was critical to know not only what worked and what didn't, but also *when* it worked—when the cash would come in from each effort.

Planning for Success

Taken together, these worksheets go a long way toward identifying who does business with you and why. In turn, this information prepares you to make the best and most effective use of your marketing and sales efforts. Ruth Owades, founder of California-based Calyx & Corolla, Inc., an upscale catalog marketer of flowers and plants, best exemplifies this process.

Chapter 5: Marketing and Product Development

Calyx & Corolla succeeded quickly because of the strong planning that Owades brought to the venture. She had worked in the mail-order and catalog business for more than a decade. Her first venture in catalog marketing, in the 1970s, was a company called Gardener's Eden, which sold quality gardening tools and supplies. She sold Gardener's Eden to a big East Coast catalog company. The experience gave her contacts and expertise in direct-mail marketing.

The idea of selling flowers and plants through the mail attracted her. The flower industry seemed ripe for innovation, and the mail-order business remained popular.

Researching the competition, Owades found several futile attempts at selling flowers through catalogs, most engineered by flower cooperatives with no feel for catalog sales.

Owades knew the catalog business well, had some money and committed herself to developing the idea.

"I wanted to start big; with so many people watching us, the risk of competition was sizable," she explains. "If it was going to work, we really had to carve out a niche quickly and establish ourselves."

She needed $2 million in start-up capital and set a goal of $3 to $4 million in revenue during Calyx & Corolla's second year of operations. She read up on writing business plans and developed her own—discovering, as she puts it, that writing a plan "uncovered the logic of the business." She dumped $150,000 of her own money into the company and tried something that might have seemed gimmicky—or, worse, might not have worked at all: she sent potential investors flowers via Federal Express, just as Calyx & Corolla customers would receive them.

Her business plan, her commitment and her Fed Ex flowers worked. Within a few weeks, she acquired all the money she needed. She hadn't done much direct-market research, betting $2 million that her ideas and her experience would make the project work. She felt confident that Calyx & Corolla could sell flowers in the $50 price range with a guarantee of overnight delivery. But she wasn't sure whether people would order flowers from a catalog instead of a flower shop.

Customer Perceptions

In many ways, catalog sales are among the most difficult to close. Catalog shoppers usually compare products and prices carefully—and slowly. The impulse purchases that drive discretionary sales like flowers rarely play a big role in catalog marketing. But Owades knew that high-income people, especially women, shop extensively by catalog. She had no problem seeing her ideal customer—someone much like herself.

So she knew that her catalog would play a pivotal role in the company's success. She called on all of her experience to lend the catalog a sense of affluence and elegance. She wanted customers to believe Calyx & Corolla had been around forever.

She intended to process orders in San Francisco. The flowers would go directly from growers to customers via overnight delivery. Thus, the company's success depended on good relations with growers and shippers.

Handling things with growers was easy. Owades found many growers looking for new ways to package product. She had no problem selling them on the idea of catalog sales.

Finding the right delivery system, however, proved more difficult. "Because of the reputation and stature it would give our business, I felt my shipper had to be Federal Express," Owades says. "Airborne, Emery and a variety of others were eager to have the business and were competitive on price but could not promise the lift capacity, the airplane space out of specific locations and a guarantee on a day-in, day-out basis to move product."

She showed good timing. Federal Express had recently made courting small businesses like Calyx & Corolla a priority. Owades set up an account with Fed Ex that assured her of on-time delivery to almost any spot in the continental U.S.

She was ready. Her first catalog went out in January 1989, and it did its job. Orders came in above Owades's projections. In 1992, its fourth year in business, the company generated profits exceeding five percent on sales of $10 million.

By 1998, Calyx & Corolla was the largest U.S. direct marketer of floral products. It mailed 12 million catalogs that same year, with sales exceeding $20 million. In 1999, they were expecting to at least double in annual revenue.

Product Development

Product development is the incremental process by which you turn an idea into a product—and thereafter, increase the product's quality and usefulness to your customer as time passes. Thus, product development has to do with existing products as well as with new; indeed, most companies develop their best new products from ones they already sell. They begin developing successor products the moment they think of the original. Truly new products are rare, and no business manager waits for a brainstorm before making improvements to existing products.

However you get to the new product, the generation of new ideas is the most interesting part of product development. In many ways, it's the most creative work of the company. As many people as reasonably possible take part in this work.

The Sources of Innovation

This includes not only employees, but customers as well. Innovations often come from routine customer comments. The company that translates its customers' wishes into products that appeal to a broad market, succeeds almost automatically.

Successful products also come from looking at what's hot in your industry, or at what your competitors do better than you do. This requires keeping tabs on your competitors; stay on the mailing lists for competitor's products and read trade journals with an eye for developments that signal new needs in your marketplace.

It's important to pursue new products even if your current lines sell well. The best kind of product development extends the interest in your products to new audiences while retaining the old. Your marketing and sales departments should welcome new products because they offer something new to talk about to customers who may have bought existing products for years. They can rekindle interest in your entire product line.

But as technology develops, it becomes more and more difficult to stay on the cutting edge in any given industry. Managers must make decisions about where their technical strengths lie, invest there and purchase other knowledge.

Historically, something like 90 percent of a company's proprietary products or technology came from in-house development and 10 percent came from outside. In the future, the breakdown may become 50-50, and the definition of "outside" may come to mean contract work, joint ventures, university research and consultants.

All this drives up costs, making product development not only the most creative but perhaps the riskiest function inside the organization. Managers must forecast how well new products will do and know when to make changes. They must also know when to abandon a project.

The Cutting Edge

For some companies, product development is everything, with ramifications multiplying throughout the enterprise. California-based Techwear Inc., for example, makes special lab coats and other clothing to control static electricity—a hazard in such industries as high-tech electronics and medicine. Owner Kay Adams sells into a market that demands better and better fabrics, and she organizes her efforts to meet that demand.

She began the company in 1987 and has used a series of business plans "almost like a notebook," as she says, to set goals and measure her success in achieving them. Her company has been profitable since 1989. Its clients include Hewlett-Packard, IBM and Boeing. When she started out,

Chapter 5: Marketing and Product Development

Adams wrote down her goals, defining her market and most promising products. Now she writes a new plan each year. Specifically, her plans include:

- A description of Techwear's industry niche;
- Financial and market objectives for the company;
- A description of Techwear's operations;
- The company's product line;
- A quick analysis of the competition;
- A description of likely customers;
- An outline of the company's marketing plan; and
- A list of company officers.

The section dealing with her product line starts with Techwear's initial product—a fabric she developed and introduced to the market—and moves through the half dozen products Techwear has since developed. Adams says this section motivates her product development efforts.

As time passes, Adams has added more detailed items to her plans—for example, marketing schedules, estimated costs, sales histories and forecasts, and complete budgets.

She talks about new product development in notes to her business plans. This is "where I usually talk about ideas and looking into developing products," she says.

"Being a small business—and woman-owned—we've never been able to acquire outside financing," Adams says, echoing a common complaint. "I've been self-financing since I started out by selling my house and using my credit cards."

Recently, Adams has focused on expanding her revenues by applying several aggressive marketing strategies, including signing up better educated and technically trained people as sales reps. The plan also identified specific territories Techwear wanted to enter, the biggest being Europe, where she thought her lab coats would sell well.

When it comes to product development, Adams often incubates ideas for a long time before she puts them in writing. But, "the fact that I put them in writing makes them more clear in my mind," she says.

"[Also], it's kind of fun to go back to earlier plans and see how naive I was…holy cow, I really believed that!" We all seem to have such hindsight experience. Documenting our ideas as we go along can help guide and define our future ones.

In 1993 Adams came up with an idea for a fabric with greatly improved static control. For the first time, she wrote product development explicitly into her planning.

Industry types told her that the material she had in mind couldn't be developed feasibly. "I set up a prototype in the office, tested it—and it worked. I kept notes in the business plan. A patent attorney told me you need to document everything," she says. She patented the new product within three months of its development and in time to generate revenue the same year. She received an additional patent in 1998. Adams thinks the product will prove a major source of revenue for her company.

Assessing Costs and Risks

New products are high-risk ventures, challenging you to anticipate and minimize the risks you undertake. The chart below assesses the riskiness of a particular new product.

	EXISTING CUSTOMERS	NEW CUSTOMERS
EXISTING PRODUCTS	Lowest Risk	Some Risk
NEW PRODUCTS	Some Risk	Highest Risk

Chapter 5: Marketing and Product Development

Smart managers expand their product line incrementally, moving in small steps from product to product and market to market.

Ask Yourself:

☐ Does the product come from a need you know your customers have? Or do you merely think it's a need? What's the evidence of that need?

☐ If specific customers want the new product more than others, can you bring them into the development process? Would they pick up some of the development costs? Would they commission the product outright?

☐ Will this new product fundamentally change your internal operations? If you have inventory under tight control, will this product interfere with that discipline?

☐ Are you counting on the quality of the product—not just value or level of service—to sell the product? If one of these three factors weighs more heavily than the others, which does?

☐ How many competing new products are in the market already? If interest centers on a competitor's product, is there room for you?

Minimizing Risk

People in product development turn an old advertising joke on themselves: "I know half of my development money is wasted. I just don't know which half."

You can minimize the loss of that money if you know that:

• You can maintain high quality with the new product;

• Customers familiar with your existing products will find the new one easy to use;

- Target customers think the product has been made just for them; and

- The product adds value to your operations without adding much new cost.

If product development is a central activity within your company, give it an equal footing with marketing, sales, operations and finance in the planning and implementation process. In this way, product development supports and helps define the core business plan.

Lagging Your Own Market

Through the 1980s, Mead Corporation's Lexis, a computer-based legal research service, dominated its field. Lexis was one of the first sophisticated and widely-used on-line services, and it made a fortune for Mead, kicking more than $50 million a year up to corporate headquarters on revenues of around $400 million. In the midst of all this promise and money, Mead decided to milk the Lexis subsidiary rather than cultivate it. The company invested little money in developing or improving Lexis services.

As a result, other data providers entered the market. By the early 1990s, Lexis was only one of many legal on-line services and it lost market share fast. In 1994, Lexis was sold and their new parent company made other strategic acquisitions of legal content providers to help them regain some of their previous market share.

"Technology and the marketplace passed them," says a former Mead manager. "Senior management was content to remain a broker of public-domain information while competitors were developing value-added services. They paid the price."

The Bottom Line

Like operations, marketing brings a particular perspective—and particular priorities—to management. Unchecked, its impulse for growth and innovation can hurt you. If you ever have doubts about allocating resources, err toward making sure that your marketing efforts remain profitable.

However you monitor its effectiveness, your marketing department should seek to remove the barriers blocking communication between you and your customers. This usually takes the form of research and information-gathering. But whatever form it takes, it needs to focus on two objectives: simplicity and sales.

Your marketing goals should seek to:

- Increase the number of potential customers who come into contact with you;

- Increase your conversion rate, so that more of these potential customers actually buy from you;

- Make sure they buy again; and

- Use this information toward product improvements and the development of new products.

Because small companies often depend on a few loyal customers to stay in business, some managers tend to pursue those sales at all costs. But marketing efforts look for future sales; they don't value existing business simply because it exists.

Other managers become so enamored of the forward-looking spin of good marketing, that they ignore all else. "A lot of people don't really want to be the president. They want to be the marketing guy," says one Maryland-based consultant.

Doing this well depends on your ability to pursue new ideas through the ordinary course of business. Small companies tend to fare best here because, being small, they remain nimble. Big or small, however, companies do poorly when turf battles erupt or factions create unwritten rules that resist change.

To get around this, managers create cross-functional teams to foster product development, calling on people from finance, marketing and operations to work together on a single new product. This can cause some confusion, but the creative upside is well worth the risk.

Ask Yourself:

☐ Are you losing market share?

☐ Are overall customer complaints trending up or down?

☐ Do you, as a group, clearly understand your customers and markets?

☐ Do you know where you are positioned in your market?

☐ Are your products and services outdated?

☐ Is your pricing appropriate and competitive?

☐ Are you regularly creating new products and offering them to existing customers?

Industry Questionnaire

This questionnaire assesses the market opportunities in the industries and markets your company serves.

Industry information may give you an idea about what your market share is. It may also tell you where developing new products may be most beneficial.

Fill out one of these for each industry in which you provide products or services at least annually.

Sources of industry information include trade associations, the U.S. Commerce Department, Standard & Poor's Industry Report, Dun & Bradstreet (many of these can be found in local libraries), annual reports of publicly held companies, on-line data services such as Lexis/Nexis and Dow Jones news services, and by talking to industry experts.

Chapter 5: Marketing and Product Development

Ask Yourself:

☐ Is this an industry that offers opportunities for your company now and in the future?

☐ Are there significant barriers to growth in this industry?

☐ Are your sales and marketing strategies focused on the right type of consumer in this kind of market sector?

☐ Does your market reward broad-based efforts or niche operations?

☐ What can you do to position the company for growth that takes advantage of its market and industry sectors? If growth prospects are limited, should you consider moving out of that market?

Go to worksheet on the following page   →

Industry Questionnaire

1. Total buying power:

   _____ number of buyers

   _____ estimated $ buying volume

2. Is this a mature or start-up industry?

3. What are the barriers, if any, when entering the industry?

4. Who are the industry leaders and why?

5. How many companies operate in this industry? Is the number increasing or decreasing?

6. Can your company expand the market in this industry?

7. Are there particular demographic factors at work in this industry?

8. Are there seasonal buying patterns inherent to this industry?

9. Can you find projections of growth trends for the industry (projections done by trade groups, security analysts, government)?

10. What are the factors that will affect demand for your product (general business conditions, technological innovation, governmental factors, customer growth)?

11. Are there any potentially adverse political, social, economic or environmental conditions?

Assessment of Competition

This worksheet provides a means to keep track of competitors' progress in the market and to learn from their successes and failures.

Being able to anticipate how a competitor will act or react can provide a significant advantage in planning your strategy.

Keeping track of your competition is more important as a sales tool than as a means of setting goals for product development or service. It is important to know what they do well, because your customers will know, even if you don't.

List all your major competitors. Use industry magazines, or trade association contacts, financial reports (like those mentioned in the Industry Questionnaire section) and news services. Some entrepreneurs even telephone competitors directly to find out about their sales volume, products and pricing policies.

Obtain their catalogs or other marketing materials and buy their products or use their services. Ask friends what they like and don't like about the competitors' product.

After reviewing public data on competitors, prepare this detailed assessment of the competition. This assessment will help identify competitors' strengths and weaknesses in products, quality, service, price, etc.

Ask Yourself:

☐ Can you counter each competitor's weakness with a strength in your product or service? How else can you turn their weaknesses to your advantage?

☐ Could they counter your weaknesses with their strengths?

☐ What parts of the market is your competition moving into? Moving away from? Do these trends have any bearing on your business?

Assessment of Competition

Competitor's Name: Location:				
Parent Company: ☐ Subsidiary ☐ Division ☐ Branch				
Product Lines(s):				
Year 200___	Sales	Net Income	Total Assets	Equity
200___				
200___				
Estimated Market Share				

Rate the following areas in order to determine major strengths and weaknesses of the competitor (suggest using "+"; "N"; "−"):

1. Name recognition _____

2. Product line _____

3. Quality _____

4. New products _____

5. Pricing _____

6. Marketing share _____

7. Financial condition _____

"+" Better than your company

"N" Neutral/About the same as your company

"−" Worse than your company

Briefly describe the competitor's reputation, competitive advantages and disadvantages and overall marketing strategy:

☐ Are your competitors more stable and better-capitalized than you are? Does this matter much in your market?

☐ How does your company's market position compare to those of your competitors? Are you a market leader or a market follower? Is there an advantage to being one or the other (which makes more money)?

Customer Communication Record

This worksheet gives customer service personnel a way to document customer comments that might be useful in product development and marketing efforts.

With so much for each employee to do every day, good ideas get lost unless they have a specific means of documentation and communication. Customer feedback is like gold, and each suggestion should be reviewed by management.

You might consider responding to these suggestions in writing. Nothing gains customer loyalty like feeling they have been heard. And customers who believe they will be heard are more likely to say something about your products. This is marketing information that many companies pay dearly to acquire.

To this end, this worksheet serves as a communications tool on several levels—and an inexpensive alternative to pricey market research.

Documenting and managing customer response is the key to using this worksheet. Give many copies to employees who talk to your customers every day and have them returned to a central location.

Encourage employees to document calls when customers express needs for products that you don't already offer them. They should also document who this customer is in terms of years they have been buying from you and dollar volume purchased.

Chapter 5: Marketing and Product Development

Have your sales force review these comments to determine whether they have heard the same sorts of requests from their customers and potential customers.

However you structure your product development efforts, have the people involved look through an archive of these reports. In a basic manner, that kind of archive can tell you whether existing customers would support—or reject—a new or modified product.

Ask Yourself:

☐ Is this suggestion one you've heard before?

☐ Does the response say anything about customer response—either pro or con—to new products you're considering?

☐ Are you following up with these suggestions and considering the products requested as a part of your new product development process?

☐ Does your marketing/product development department take these suggestions as seriously as ones developed through other means?

☐ Do you give credit to customer service reps when products that were suggested through them become company success stories?

Customer Communication Record

To: **Product Development Dept.**   Date _____

        Marketing Dept.   Time _____

From: **Customer Service Dept.**

    _____

We received a   ☐ call   ☐ letter   ☐ e-mail

_____
(customer name, address & phone)

has been a customer for _____ years, and has purchased $ _____ from us in total, $ _____ of which has been this year. The main products they purchase from us are:

_____

Their concerns were:

Comments from sales force:

Product Sales by Marketing Method

Marketing a product often costs more than the manufacturing of the product itself. Ineffective marketing efforts result in failed products, even if the products themselves meet every other criteria for product success.

To spend marketing dollars most effectively, the company must know what works, spend its money on things that work, and eliminate or modify efforts that are less successful. This is a constant process. A marketing method that has worked for years may decline, while another type of effort may suddenly become more important.

Hence, it's important to determine not only what the sales were by product, but also which of the company's sales efforts made the customer aware of the product, decide to order it, and place an order by phone, mail or in person, to the company directly, or through one of its other distribution channels.

Most companies use a variety of marketing methods. This worksheet lists many of them across the top. To begin, list your products and the total dollar volume sales attributed to each in the first and last columns on the sheet. Then determine how much of your business is new and how much is from customers who have done business with you before.

All of the new business should be broken down into how the customer first heard about you: by direct mail, the phone book, telemarketing or an advertisement (television, radio or print media); through someone who sells for you (such as a retail establishment) or one of your sales reps; from word of mouth from another satisfied customer or some other channel.

In the top left portion of the box, list the actual dollars attributed to that type of marketing.

Once all the boxes are filled in, use the bottom right corner of the box to calculate the percentage of business attributed to that effort by dividing the total sales by effort by the new sales total.

Product Sales By Marketing Method
(last full year)

New Sales $/(% of total sales)

Product	Direct Mail	Telephone Book	Tele-marketing	Advertising	Distributors
TOTALS					

	($/%)				(% of total sale)
Sales Force	Referral	Other	A New Sale Total	B Repeat Business	Total[1] Sales (A + B)

[1]The total by product comes from the $ sales column of the *Sales By Product and Customer* worksheet for last year

Ask Yourself:

☐ Is one type of marketing responsible for most of your sales dollars? In total or just in one type of product?

☐ Is this because your marketing expertise is limited or because you've tried other methods and this is the one that works?

☐ Are most methods of marketing represented to some extent, or are many boxes blank?

☐ Could you use other marketing methods that you aren't currently using?

☐ Is a disproportionate amount of your business either repeat or new? (You may be missing new opportunities if it is mostly repeat. However, if it is mostly new, it may mean that customers are not satisfied enough to return.)

☐ Does your marketing say anything about new products you haven't considered?

☐ Why aren't you producing a requested product now? There's little demand? It's too difficult to begin the process?

☐ Who should follow up ongoing communications?

Product Development Proposal

This worksheet helps you consider and document the merits of product development ideas from any source: your customers, your employees, distributors, etc.

Just as with important customer feedback, unless you capture new ideas for products that come from employees, meetings, reading materials, etc., they will get lost. However, it is important to have a way to collect these ideas, and equally important to have a forum for discussion and decision making. Set up a committee to explore new product ideas, with employees from all parts of the company in attendance. If employees feel their ideas will be heard, they will be more likely to bring them to you.

Many companies also give employees a percentage of the profits from any product development their ideas have launched.

Like the Customer Communication Record, this is primarily a communications tool—though its application to product development is clearer. Hand copies of these forms to all employees and ask that they be returned to you or to a central location. Express your enthusiasm for product development and let employees know you want them to be active participants in the process.

When new ideas emerge, help employees do preliminary research by assisting them in filling out the questions asked in this worksheet, especially in regard to competition.

Ask Yourself:

- ☐ Is this product one we could sell easily along with other products we currently sell?

- ☐ Does it have a large market potential?

- ☐ Would this product be costly to produce?

- ☐ Does it have direct competition? Could we produce a superior product?

- ☐ How did this idea originate? From an existing product? From a gap in the market? From an unresolved customer need?

- ☐ Does the origin of the idea say anything about *other* new products you might consider?

Product Development Proposal

Product Description:

Is this product related to products we currently sell?

Who will use the products?

Could we sell this product to current customers or is this a new market?

Estimated market potential:

How will the product be used?

Who else offers this product or one similar to it?

Product Name	Competitor Name	Price	Strengths	Weaknesses

Product Development Checklist

Even if product development is routine at your company, it is easy to realize at the last moment that some important step was missed—packaging not ordered, price discounts not set, no plan for notifying current customers, and many other common missing pieces that can undo an otherwise well-thought-out plan.

This worksheet helps you make sure you have covered all the important steps in the product development process.

Once you have decided to pursue development of a product, there are many decisions to be made and things that must be done between idea and prototype.

This checklist gives some of the many items. Chief among these: projected ship date and initial quantity. Experience is the best guide to make these decisions, but most small companies try to schedule twice the normal production time to new products and keep early batches to the smallest, cost-effective unit.

While production and operations usually require the most attention during new product development, don't ignore marketing efforts. Especially if the new product moves away from or beyond traditional markets, more time and effort will have to go into sales and promotion.

Some owners and managers fall into the trap of thinking that they can sell a product *after* they've made it. Try to keep the production and marketing functions as simultaneous as you can.

Meet with your product development team regularly and review the checklist. Use it as a record of each step and add items that are relevant to your company.

Product Development Checklist

Product_____

Projected Ship Date _____

Initial Quantity _____

1. Production
   - ☐ Design specifications
   - ☐ Materials required
   - ☐ Person-hours required
   - ☐ Temporary help required
   - ☐ Equipment required

2. Miscellaneous Production
   - ☐ Storage requirements
   - ☐ Other packaging

3. Other Costs
   - ☐ Licensing fees

4. Order Entry
   - ☐ Pricing discounts
   - ☐ Shipping schedule
   - ☐ Distribution

5. Marketing
   - ☐ Marketing research
   - ☐ Marketing plan
   - ☐ Pricing
   - ☐ Methods
     - ☐ Stuffers
     - ☐ Direct mail
     - ☐ Telemarketing
     - ☐ Sales reps
       - ☐ Commission schedules
   - ☐ Packaging with other products

6. General
   - ☐ Set sales goals
   - ☐ Determine costs
   - ☐ Calculate breakevens

Comments

Ask Yourself:

☐ Have you discussed the new product and its development with all employees who will play a role in the production, marketing or sales of this product?

☐ Did you include their input to make this process as smooth as possible?

☐ Did you set a realistic timetable to get everything done?

☐ Will you have sales made as soon as the new product is ready to ship? How do booked sales change the initial quantities you'll produce?

☐ Have internal production and operations functions gotten ahead of external sales and marketing functions? If so, what can you do to bring the two together?

Product Development Forecast

This worksheet reasonably estimates the sales of this product during the first three years and estimates costs associated with this product to determine how soon you can expect a profit.

Sales are very difficult to project for any newly developed product. They are more projectable when the product is similar to one you already make, or to a market you already sell to.

Costs may also be difficult to separate out.

This is a very simple formula for looking at whether or not a new product is feasible financially. Profitability is a very important component, but there are other considerations about product development. It is essential to continue the processes of development so as not to stagnate your company. You may also need to develop products to fill gaps for customers in order to retain other business.

The top half of the worksheet helps you estimate sales by looking at market potential and your possible share of that market.

The bottom half helps project the costs associated with the development of the product, and the ongoing costs for materials and labor that will continue over the life of the product.

Ask Yourself:

☐ Looking at the two shaded boxes on the worksheet, is the selling price adequate to cover your costs and leave enough for an adequate profit margin?

☐ Even if the product would be profitable soon, are the out-of-pocket development costs still prohibitive for your company?

☐ How do the projected sales and costs of this product compare to your other products? To your most successful product?

☐ Do your projections seem to mirror the actual performance of other new products you've developed or that your market has embraced?

☐ If the product costs 10 percent more to develop, would you proceed? If it costs 10 percent less?

Product Development
Sales and Cost Forecast
Product _____

	Sales	This year	Next year	3rd year
A	Total Market			
B	Expected % of Market (expressed as decimal point)			
C	Projected Number of Units to be Sold (A x B)			
D	Selling Price		▨	
E	Total $ Volume Expected			

Costs	1st year (development)	Next year (ongoing)
Cost of Goods Sold Materials Direct labor Research & Development		
Sales & Marketing		
Overhead Indirect labor Overhead allocation		
TOTALS	A	A
Projected # of Units to be Sold	B	B
Unit cost (A ÷ B)	C	C ▨

Business Plans to Game Plans

Chapter 6:

Sales and Customer Service

If marketing is mostly theory, sales are mostly action. Selling is one-to-one contact with the customer, talking, listening and taking the order. Customer service is about getting another order.

Sales and customer service are in some ways simple and direct. But in their simplicity lies the difficulty: they offer no place to hide. It happens here, or it doesn't happen at all.

Some CEOs come from sales and love the showmanship and one-to-one contact. In fact, a study done by Sales and Marketing Executives International in 1998 showed that a company's average annual increase in sales is generally higher if the CEO came from a sales background than from any other discipline. Others find this area a challenge.

Sales and Profitability

Determine the profitability of your products and identify your customers before you do anything else. You can't set up appropriate sales efforts or sales compensation programs if you don't. If sales are profitable, the next step is getting to know your best customers. How can you make their experience with your company better, keep them, increase their business, as well as find others like them?

Bill Miller, a project manager with the PricewaterhouseCoopers marketing consulting group Management Horizons, works primarily in the retail merchandise industry with clients like Sears, Pier One Imports, the Warner Brothers and Disney store chains and the Limited—a sector with complex customer and product mixes.

Retailers often use benchmarks, but Miller says that making generalizations about which benchmarks to use can be dangerous. "The benchmarks you'll use will vary too much by product and industry," he says.

Management Horizons distributes questionnaires, surveys individual customers, convenes focus groups and interviews people about their buying habits, what people look for in clothes and other products, where they go first when they enter a store and why.

In retail sales, marketing consultants check every aspect of the business from the design of the store to lighting, display and the appearance of the clerks. Miller points out that stores in the Gap and Limited chains are very clean not because managers enforce personal manias for cleanliness but because market research indicates that customers value clean stores.

Great companies successfully balance customer needs with their own growth and profit objectives. And these success stories don't happen by accident. The companies look for sales that generate the most money for the longest time—quality sales.

Sales and Customer Service

Great service is a key to quality sales, and studies of consumer and corporate buying habits consistently reinforce this notion. In some markets, customers rate service more highly than quality when choosing one product over another.

Market research can tell you how well you serve your customers by collecting information and adapting this knowledge to your markets. The expectations of your customers will increase every year, no matter what industry you are in. How often do you overpromise and underdeliver? Make sure your market research helps your company to:

- Identify and define customer expectations regarding service;

- Translate expectations into clear, deliverable service features;

- Arrange efficient, responsive and integrated service delivery systems and structures;

- Monitor and control service quality and performance; and

- Provide quick, cost-effective response to customers' needs.

Creating sales opportunities is a marketing responsibility. If, for example, you enhance your product's usefulness to your customer by offering valuable benefits from a related line, you create an interested listener ready to hear more about your products. Each time you propose an innovative approach to a real need, you create a sales opportunity. In order to do these things, your sales force has to know how customers utilize your products.

A New Approach for the Airlines

In mid-1999, the Air Transport Association, the trade group of America's major airlines, released a plan called Customers First. The voluntary plan culminated after talks between the airlines, Congress and the Department of Transportation on the lack of a customer service focus from many of the airlines. It has subsequently been adopted by most U.S. airline companies and will be available to consumers via Web sites and at airport ticketing areas. The major reforms to airline customer service are these: airlines will tell passengers about the lowest fares available, will notify customers of delays and cancelations as early as possible, will make a greater attempt to find passengers' lost luggage and will do a better job meeting passenger needs during long waits aboard an aircraft.

One of the first to adopt these procedures was Southwest Airlines. The Dallas-based carrier has been in business since 1971 and has the airline industry's best cumulative consumer satisfaction record—a measurement kept and published by the Department of Transportation. Their mission statement reads as follows:

> *The mission of Southwest Airlines is dedication to the highest quality of Customer Service delivered with a sense of warmth, friendliness, individual pride, and Company Spirit.*

Southwest covers its customer service promise to passengers in an 18-page booklet. At the end, after reiterating its mission statement, Southwest continues:

> *The information in this document is intended to show you that, regardless of the circumstances that may arise during your flight, we have already thought about your safety, your well-being, your pocketbook, and your expectations. You see, we are not only here to get you from point "A" to point "B," we are here to help when things aren't going quite right for you or for us.*

Southwest knows that uncontrollable and unexpected situations will arise: weather delays, problems at terminals, etc. But it also knows that customers will look to Southwest to make sure these problems are minimized or create the least inconvenience for them. This airline has taken a proactive stance toward serving customers, even when problems are not the airline's fault. They anticipate problems and worked out schematic solutions before the unexpected happens.

Focus on Your Customers

Focus groups provide a simple but very effective way to get an idea about what your customers think about your industry and your product. Attract customers or potential customers with the inducement of small amounts of cash or sample products. Interview them and describe your product or service—or, better yet, show them—and ask for feedback. Watch as well as listen to the reaction.

Review the results of focus groups with as many managers as feasible. This educates your staff about the problems the product will face—and gives your company the chance to respond. Staff needs to see customers talking about what they want. Seeing this response arouses their attention, making innovation more likely.

Set up interviews by phone, mail or in person with targeted customers. Send out written surveys to larger groups of customers or potential customers. Find out how these customers consider quality, value and service in relation to your product. Ask them to describe their responses in some detail.

Look for information on price ranges and barriers, format or style preferences, service requirements and probable buying patterns.

Find out how customers perceive your competition. Another point to explore: how do your customers get information about competitors and their products—advertising, direct mail, word of mouth?

Analyze the responses with a focus on what features your product should have and what would make it more attractive. Find out where you outperform or lag your competition.

Illustrate your results in graphic form and publicize them within your company. Let your coworkers know what customers think of their work and what they look for in the future.

Customer research also seeks to learn what motivates people to buy what you sell. In this process, anything that tracks sales in a detailed way helps you—a major reason why big retailers offer their own credit cards, encourage catalog orders, code their register receipts and have you register at their Web site. It's also why direct mail marketers offer free gifts, and why home shopping and computer on-line services make marketers' mouths water.

You can't control marketplace forces, but you can minimize your marketing risks. When you own a reliable base of data about your customers and their tendencies, you can sell selectively to people most likely to buy a particular product. If you know that middle aged Philadelphia men buy red ties in February, you may know all you need to know in order to effectively use your marketing and sales budget.

Changing the Mint

The U.S. Mint has annual revenues of approximately $2.5 billion and employs over 2,200 people. The Mint's job is producing U.S. coins and protecting Fort Knox. In 1994, Philip Diehl became Director of the Mint and decided to make some dramatic changes in its operations and customer service.

But it was not easy to make changes in a bureaucratic institution like the Mint—in fact, in some ways it was discouraged. The Office of Management and Budget (OMB) of the U.S. Government must approve expenditures, and it generally doesn't approve expenditures of such items as customer service surveying. So Diehl decided to do the research himself by attending the same trade shows as his customers—the coin collectors. He was able to identify the Mint's biggest customer service problems and fix them. He set a goal that the Mint would process 95 percent of its orders within six weeks. Today, the Mint delivers 95 percent of its orders within two weeks. Additional goals included telephone calls being answered in seconds instead of minutes and mail being handled in days instead of months.

Diehl made customer service a priority for the agency and discovered how his customers viewed his product and service. The Mint now uses its Web site for e-commerce and as a method for judging customer satisfaction in real time.

The Right Person for the Job

Your sales people and your customer service reps can be unpopular in your organization; they are often the bearers of bad news from customers. It is hard to come to terms with the fact that your product may not be meeting all of the customer needs, that your competitors may be producing a better product cheaper than you are.

Pick the right people for this job—not everyone can do it. Sales people thrive on contact with people, so make sure they have lots of contact with others inside your organization, as well as outside. Expect some "us against them" problems, especially if you primarily pay sales people on commission. A commission system makes salespeople very vulnerable to the performance of the rest of the company, so that one group of employees could be preventing another from maximizing their income. Likewise, sales people are typically the most highly compensated employees, often making more money than the CEO. This is appropriate because this income may be inconsistent, varying widely between one year and the next due to changes in the market.

There was always jealousy between sales people and other employees in my company when it came to compensation and general attention. There was a constant need to re-educate people about the risk and reward aspect of a sales person's work.

Sales people also often receive trips and other perks for high performance. I found that the best technique to minimize problems was to keep paying lots of attention to and rewarding the sales people, while training the sales people to give lots of credit to others in the company. Some sales people understand and acknowledge this relationship naturally, while others need to be trained to appreciate what the rest of the staff does to make their job easier.

Most sales are based equally on belief in a product and trust in the person selling it. People do business with people, not demographic surveys. Customers want to—and have to—believe in what and from whom they're buying. You have a lot of control over whether they believe.

An irony of business is that your customers' perception of your business may rely almost solely on their contacts with some of your lowest paid employees: your customer service representatives. And the reality is that how these employees feel about you and your company may determine how the customers feel about you.

Set high standards for professionalism, etiquette, ethics and positive attitude. These things matter throughout your company, but having a bad day probably won't be a disaster in other areas. In customer service, it will. Keep good records about how many calls come in, the average time it takes to handle a call completely, but efficiently, as well as the common customer questions and issues. Also keep track of your absenteeism and employee complaints.

Make it easy and fun for your customer service reps to make it easy and fun for your customers. One of the best things we did at my company was to create quizzes on product information and other information the customer service reps were frequently asked about by customers. We awarded prizes and announced winners in the employee newsletter.

Train everyone working with customers on how to handle difficult situations. With a few tools for dealing with angry customers, this job is made much easier.

Many telephone customer service reps sit in front of a computer screen and take orders as they are placed. They can also track shipments and change customer information while they are on the phone. Almost every aspect of a product can and should be available on the computer without having to transfer calls or leave the area.

Using the Whole Approach

Austin-based Whole Foods Market describes customers as "our most important stakeholders in our business and the lifeblood of our business." The 20-year-old company has about 90 stores with 14,000 employees under six different store names throughout the U.S. It is known for selling the highest quality natural and organic products available.

Each new employee team member is hired directly by the store where that individual will be working, and all training is done at the store level. There are two full days of orientation and training, discussing products available, merchandising, customer service philosophy and conflict resolution. After the initial training, each team member is part of a buddy system where key people are assigned to partner with new employees for additional one-to-one training and mentoring. Over time, individuals looking for promotional opportunities within the store can take mini-series courses on leadership.

Each store has a distinct personality that matches its serving community. Store purchasing is based on the needs of that community. Team members are eligible for gain sharing based on sales in four-week cycles. Teams also meet every four weeks to discuss problems to be solved and opportunities for increased sales. To emphasize the value of each employee, company policy says that no one person can make more than 10 times the average employee's salary, including the CEO.

Their often-quoted measures of success include customer satisfaction, team member excellence and happiness, return on capital investment, improvement in the state of the environment and community support.

They have pursued an aggressive acquisition strategy over the past five years, but hope to double the number to 200 by 2004. Their constant focus on quality and service has paid off. They are the market leader in natural foods retailing with sales four times greater than their competitor.

Tracking Sales

Keep meticulous track of all your sales and categorize them in different ways—top products, what you sell, whom you sell to and what you sell them, where you sell what you sell, what you sell profitably and what you don't. Keep track of these statistics in real time, which allows you to keep better track of inventory. But you still need to set aside time to determine what these numbers mean in terms of marketing and sales activities.

Have monthly meetings to discuss the implications of the sales numbers, quarterly sales strategy planning retreats and then annual meetings with most of the management staff. Discuss changes you want to make to the product line as a result of what you learn from the sales figures. Use the annual meeting as a time to discuss what customers you want to retain and who is no longer profitable for you. The best way my company found to discourage unprofitable customers was to raise prices.

We often used the quarterly meetings to discuss the performance of the sales staff and their compensation. Sales compensation is always an issue—whether you are paying them too much or too little, whether enough of their compensation is based on commission or too little, and whether you provide effective incentives for making the right kind of sales. We tried a variety of methods, some with better success than others, but always found we needed to tie compensation to profitability. Otherwise, what worked for the sales person didn't necessarily work for the company.

It is estimated that the average small company loses 20 percent of its customers each year, so you should probably aim for 25 percent to 33 percent of your sales to come each year from new customers in order to grow. That leaves two-thirds to three-fourths of your sales to come from customers that have done business with you before. Both kinds of sales are essential to the prosperity of your business. New sales bring increases to your top line and help grow your company. Sales from existing customers are the most profitable.

Communicating Sales Data to Employees

Share overall sales for the company and sales by product line with all employees. I believe it is their right to know; they can often find ways to improve sales and profitability when they know the score. Company success is typically measured on sales volume or on sales volume increases. It is a point of pride for most employees to know and share their company's annual revenue. While many employees don't understand profitability or are skeptical of its accurate measurement, sales volume is a number to which most can clearly relate.

The Bottom Line

The goal of your sales and customer service programs is clear: get the initial sale and keep the customer coming back for your product or service again. Acquire and keep the best employees you can in this area—employees who enjoy working with people and solving problems, and who aren't easily deterred from their mission. Do your best to keep these employees happy and help educate other employees on their vital role.

Get out and meet your best customers yourself. Put yourself in the customers' shoes as often as possible and don't rationalize problems with your product or service. Learn to appreciate customer feedback.

Celebrate sales increases with all employees. Increases signify that you and your employees have produced something of value for your customers; and fostering the opportunity for your staff to take pride in their success is important. Sales dollars are the customers' way of expressing appreciation for what your company does.

Don't be satisfied with your sales and customer service effort until you can answer "yes" to all of these questions:

- Are you satisfied with your revenue growth?
- Are all of your product sales profitable?
- Can you identify customers or groups of customers whose business is not profitable for you?
- Are you satisfied with your plan to sell or deliver product via the Internet?
- Do you spend time with your sales people, one-to-one?
- Do you spend time with your top customers, one-to-one?
- Are your sales and customer service people superstars?

Dollar Sales: Month to Month

This is a simple and straightforward way to look at what your actual sales are month by month, compared to projections, by product. A lot of information is contained in a very simple worksheet:

This enables you to see what is and isn't working, what products sales show an increase in sales and what products may need changes in direction in order to remain viable.

The worksheet shows actual sales figures compared to sales projections by month, and determines average sales by month.

Dollar Sales Month To Month For _____

(Month/Year)

Product	Goal for Current Mo.	1 Jan.	2 Feb.	3 Mar.	4 April	5 May
Totals						

6 June	7 July	8 Aug.	9 Sept.	10 Oct.	11 Nov.	12 Dec.	Total Year-to-date Sales	Avg. Sales by Mo.[1]

[1]Divide total year-to-date Sales By Current Month number.

List all of your products, or product lines in the left column. Take the projections developed in the Dollar Sales Projections by Product worksheet, and add those in the second column.

Then, on a monthly basis, add in your actual sales dollars by product.

If you have records of past years, make copies of these worksheets and plot the numbers for these years. Total all sales by month and put that number in the total column that is next to last. Finally, divide this number by the total number of months for which you have sales figures (divide by 12 if you have numbers for the whole year) to get an average dollar sales figure by month.

Ask Yourself:

☐ Do you see any cyclicality by product?

☐ Can you structure your sales and marketing efforts to take advantage of sales trends?

☐ For which products are your goals more than your actual sales?

☐ Is this because you were overly optimistic when making projections?

☐ For which products do actual sales exceed goals? Is this expected to continue, or is it due to a particular marketing effort?

Product Sales by Customer

A goal of every company should be to sell as much of each type of product as possible to every customer it acquires. This calculation is an indication of how many dollars each customer spends with your company. Looking at three years of data lets you see whether customers are spending more on average than they did two years ago, or less.

Since so much money is spent just letting potential customers know that you exist, additional sales to existing customers are a very profitable business. Every company should have a plan for selling more product to existing customers. This worksheet can help you track your working plan.

Chapter 6: Sales and Customer Service

The following page calculates your dollar volume per customer over the past three years.

Use the same three-year lists of products and total dollars per product you developed in the Dollar Sales Month to Month worksheet for the first two columns (A and B) of this worksheet.

Add the total number of customers that buy each product in column C.

Divide column B numbers by column C numbers to get column D.

Was this exercise difficult because so many customers buy more than one product or product type, or are your customers generally customers for one type of product only? (If you had a difficult time segregating customers by product, then the total company numbers at the bottom of the page will be most meaningful for you.)

Ask Yourself:

☐ What products bring in the highest dollar volume per customer?

☐ What products increase the dollar volume per customer numbers every year?

☐ Are these increases due to price fluctuation, or has the number of units sold to each of these customers gone up? (The shaded box in the very bottom right of the worksheet becomes one of your key indicators. Measured over time, this will tell you if you are increasing sales dollars per customer.)

☐ Is your customer base shrinking or growing?

☐ Do a few customers account for a specific portion of a particular product's sales? If so, what can you do to take optimum advantage of that connection?

Product Sales By Customer

	Two Years Ago		
A Product	B $ Sales	C # of Customers	D $ Per Customer (B ÷ C)
Total Company			

Last Year			This Year		
B $ Sales	C # of Customers	D $ Per Customer (B ÷ C)	B $ Sales	C # of Customers	D $ Per Customer (B ÷ C)

Top 25 Dollar-Volume Customers

This worksheet determines who are the customers that purchase the most dollar volume for this year and last year.

It is often useful to ask whether the types of people who buy from you have anything in common. Grouping types of customers will allow you to do this. Look at this worksheet for interesting patterns in customer type. For instance, your customers may be demographically similar with respect to age, income range, gender or profession.

Location is important for the same reason. There may be something about your product that is particularly appealing to people in cities, warm climates or newly developed areas.

Assemble a list of all of your customers for the past two years, and rank order the top 25 each year by dollar volume purchased.

On this worksheet, list your top customers starting with the customers who did the most business with you this year. List your most significant customers, even if you have fewer than 25. If you try to keep more than 25 customers on the list, it usually becomes difficult to analyze effectively.

Also list the various types of customer you serve (if you have any statistics like SIC codes that segregate customers in meaningful ways) and their location (possibly by city, state or zip code).

How significant is this group of customers to your business? To find out, first divide the total at the bottom of the page that adds up the sales volume of your top customers by the total sales of the company for that same period of time.

This group of customers accounted for _____ percent of the company's total sales.

Secondly, divide the number of significant customers you listed on this page with your total number of customers.

This group of customers makes up _____ percent of the company's total customer base.

Top 25 Dollar-Volume Customers
(ranked by $ Volume)

Name	Customer Type	Location	$ Volume This Year	$ Volume/Ranking Last Year
1.				
2.				
3.				
4.				
5.				
6.				
7.				
8.				
9.				
10.				
11.				
12.				
13.				
14.				
15.				
16.				
17.				
18.				
19.				
20.				
21.				
22.				
23.				
24.				
25.				

- ☐ Are your most significant customers primarily comprised of a specific type of customer? And if so, can you find ways to sell to more of these individuals?

- ☐ Are your most significant customers centered in a particular location? And if so, can you find ways to market more heavily in this area?

- ☐ Are you retaining your top dollar volume customers over time?

- ☐ Are you acquiring new, significant customers?

Top Selling Products

This exercise helps you determine what products sell the highest number of units and bring in the most revenue.

If you have only one product, this will be easy. If you have more than one, it is important to know which ones your customers like best. But even if you only have five, your top product is probably the one for which you should consider developing add-on or similar products.

You may also wish to analyze how you market these successful sellers and see if you can make similar efforts with other products.

Assemble a list of the sales in units and dollars of your products for the past two years. Rank them from top to bottom on the worksheet, starting with the product that sold the greatest dollar volume last year.

Complete the worksheet by filling in the projected and actual units and dollars for the two-year period.

Ask Yourself:

- ☐ For which products were your actual numbers above or below your projections? What caused the variances: the projections or your performance?

- ☐ What products increased your sales volume? Why?

Top Selling Products

Product	Last Year				This Year			
	Units		Dollars		Units		Dollars	
	Projected	Actual	Projected	Actual	Projected	Actual	Projected	Actual
Totals:								

- ☐ What products decreased your sales volume? Why?

- ☐ Do the trends up or down in sales suggest long-term changes in your market? Or can circumstances within your company explain the trends?

- ☐ Are your top products related in any way? Could you create further products related to these? Could you market other products with these?

Sales by Salesperson

This worksheet helps you look at how well your sales people are performing over time. It looks at sales both in terms of the individual salesperson and in terms of whether sales are linked to new customers or existing customers.

You may choose to do separate worksheets per product or product group if you sell a variety of types of products.

This will allow you to compare the performance of sales people and help you better coach or incentivize them to a different balance of new or existing customer sales.

Compile a list of all of your sales people in the left column. Then add in your projected and actual sales for this year—you may wish to do this each month using year-to-date figures—separating sales between those to new customers and those to existing customers. Do this same exercise again for last year. You may wish to use year-to-date figures in this area of the worksheet in order to have comparable data in both sections.

You could also do the same analysis looking at products that have been introduced over the past 12 months.

Ask Yourself:

☐ Are some sales people clearly outperforming others? Are some sales people clearly underperforming when you know their potential?

☐ Are you satisfied with the mix of new customers and existing customers?

☐ Is the performance of your sales people increasing or decreasing over time? By each individual? For the group?

☐ Were your projections uniformly too optimistic?

☐ Is your sales compensation plan appropriate for the sales volume brought in for each salesperson?

☐ What percentage of total sales is brought in by each salesperson?

Go to worksheet on the following page   →

Sales By Salesperson

Name of Salesperson	This Year			
	New Customers		Existing Customers	
	Proj $	Actual $	Proj $	Actual $

Last Year			
New Customers		Existing Customers	
Proj $	Actual $	Proj $	Actual $

Customer Service Key Indicators

This worksheet helps you monitor the workload and productivity of the customer service representatives and the department as a whole. It's a diagnostic tool.

Keeping the pulse of activity in customer service can be a general indication of how well the company is running. This worksheet and any other measurements of customer satisfaction are key to a general determination of operational efficiency. The worksheet can be used to track the productivity of the individuals who answer your telephones.

Posting these measurements will give rise to the natural competition between individuals, especially for sales dollars.

List each customer service representative by name and, if your telephone equipment and computer equipment will allow, enter the number of calls each has answered. Also enter the percentage of time spent on the phone, the percentage of time they are not available to take calls and the dollar volume of sales per sales rep.

At the bottom of the worksheet, tally the number of calls in each category over the past two years by month.

The bottom half of this worksheet is a good indicator for sales. It seems the more calls received, the higher the sales dollars for the month. If complaint calls have increased, it may be a measure of problems in shipping or in the quality of the product.

Ask Yourself:

- ☐ Are numbers of calls answered going up or down?
- ☐ Are order calls going up faster than the number of calls in general?
- ☐ Are complaint calls increasing?
- ☐ How do the numbers of calls you receive relate to the various products you make or market sectors you serve?

Customer Service Key Indicators

for _____
(month/year)

Name _____		
	This mo.	YTD
Calls answered	_____	____
% time on phone	_____	____
% time not available	_____	____
$ Sales per terminal	_____	____

Name _____		
	This mo.	YTD
Calls answered	_____	____
% time on phone	_____	____
% time not available	_____	____
$ Sales per terminal	_____	____

Name _____		
	This mo.	YTD
Calls answered	_____	____
% time on phone	_____	____
% time not available	_____	____
$ Sales per terminal	_____	____

Name _____		
	This mo.	YTD
Calls answered	_____	____
% time on phone	_____	____
% time not available	_____	____
$ Sales per terminal	_____	____

TOTALS

Last Year	Jan.	Feb.	Mar.	April	May	June	July	Aug.	Sept.	Oct.	Nov.	Dec.
Calls received												
Calls answered												
Calls abandoned %												
Average talk time												
Calls categorized: Orders												
Inquiries												
Complaints												

This Year	Jan.	Feb.	Mar.	April	May	June	July	Aug.	Sept.	Oct.	Nov.	Dec.
Calls received												
Calls answered												
Calls abandoned %												
Average talk time												
Calls categorized: Orders												
Inquiries												
Complaints												

☐ How do per-unit revenue or profitability numbers relate to customer service contacts?

☐ Can you find ways to reward superperformers in terms of numbers of calls taken and sales volume?

Customer Service Survey

This survey assesses your customers' opinions of your products and services. Data gathered here can help you improve your service to current customers. It may also help you lure back customers you have lost or prevent the loss of other customers.

Send this survey to each demographic group of customers. Try to send at least 50 surveys per group, if possible. You might select demographic groups by sales volume, by product type or by particular distribution method.

You may only get back a small percentage of surveys sent. You can increase this response rate if you give customers a reason to return it—a discount on their next order or a free premium. The larger the number returned, the better the data you have from which to draw conclusions. You might consider asking the form to be returned directly to the company president by including a self-addressed, stamped envelope. You will get a better response and the responses will be more meaningful if customers believe the president of the company will read their survey comments.

You can also do a survey by e-mail or at your Web site, especially if you give an incentive to fill it out.

Tabulate responses by taking each question individually, totaling the 1-10 score received, and dividing that number by the number of surveys received with that question answered. This will give you an average score for each question.

Distribute your scores throughout the company. Congratulate yourself on scores of 8-10. Continue to improve on scores of 5-7. Consider scores of 4 or under to require immediate attention focused on those areas of

Customer Service Survey

Please help us provide outstanding service by rating us in the following categories.
10= best

Question	1-10	Comments
Telephone calls are answered promptly		
Customer service reps are helpful and knowledgeable		
Your orders are filled correctly		
You are informed about new products or product changes		
We are easy to do business with		
Items ordered are received in good condition		
Orders are received promptly		
We deal with problems efficiently and effectively		
Orders are complete and correct when received		
We offer good value for the price paid		
Products are easy to use		
Billing is accurate		
Credit terms are clear		
We provide timely responses to your requests		
What new products would you like to see us produce (include changes to our current product line)?		
What can we do to improve our relationship with you?		
Comments about other areas we missed in this survey:		

☐   There is more to say and I would like you to telephone me. The best time to call is _____ .

Name and Company Name (optional)

_____

your company. Put together interdepartmental task forces to devise action plans in order to increase your levels of service.

Particularly consider the remarks in the comments sections. Call any customers who requested one, and do so within a week of receiving their completed survey. Send a thank you note to all customers who filled in their name at the bottom of the survey.

This survey should be done annually and results trended over time.

Ask Yourself:

☐ Is customer service getting the priority it deserves in your company?

☐ Are most of your scores in the 8-10 range?

☐ Was there a similarity in customer comments, particularly by demographic groups?

☐ What can you do to immediately change customer perception for the better?

☐ Are your scores trended up or down over time?

Sales Report to Employees

This worksheet—a communications tool—provides employees with a way to look at sales and receive an analysis meaningful to them about what the numbers mean.

Use this form as you would the Financial Report to Employees. Circulate it once a month and discuss it at regular meetings. You can use this report as an opportunity to congratulate outstanding performers on the sales team and encourage everyone to get involved in sales and promotion.

Fill in this worksheet with information from the Dollar Sales Month to Month worksheet and others in this section.

Provide a simple analysis at the bottom of the page by determining what products are up or down from projections and translating the importance of these changes for your employees.

240   Attach the important worksheets developed in this section.

TO: All Employees

Sales Report To Employees
for _____
(month/year)

Product	Proj MTD $	Actual MTD $	Proj YTD $	Actual YTD $
Total Company				

Comments:

Products above projections:

Products below projections:

We were (above/below) projections for the month by _____ %.

New accounts this month:

Attachments: Dollar Sales by Product, Unit Sales, Top Products/Top Customers

Ask Yourself:

- [ ] Are you where you expected to be in sales for the company overall, on a year-to-date basis?

- [ ] Are some products doing much better than expected? Why?

- [ ] Are some products behind expectations?

- [ ] Are there reasons that can be corrected?

- [ ] What can each employee focus on to improve sales?

- [ ] Do employees understand the marketing concepts and numbers used in this report? If not, how long would it take them to learn enough to use this?

CHAPTER 7:

OPERATIONS

Operations oversees production, quality control, inventory, shipping, facility maintenance, relations with vendors and suppliers, and information services. In all of this, the goal for operations is to achieve the highest possible efficiency, making the best use of equipment and human resources—in other words, to reduce costs without damaging sales.

Thus, operations is the natural choice for ensuring that your business reaches your goals for gross margin. Operations implementation entails looking at ways to constantly improve your process, shorten production time and heighten quality. It means constant measuring and setting new standards.

Benchmarking

For obvious reasons, benchmarking is a popular tool in assessing the performance of operations. It's straightforward and, properly focused, highlights the important tasks that operations must accomplish.

But benchmarking doesn't automatically set the right goals. Would Federal Express have built its business with benchmarks tied to the performance of the U.S. Postal Service? It might have offered four day delivery to beat the Postal Service by one day. But instead, it targeted a higher standard and gave us overnight delivery, forcing the Postal Service to measure itself against a very competitive service.

The point here is that market-based benchmarks—those pegged to the performance of your competitors—serve as minimum standards, not as the be-all and end-all. They work for starters, but only if you can't come up with better standards against which to measure your own performance. Identify and aim for best-case performance standards, irrespective of what your competition does.

It's easy to find performance standards for operations. How well your operations people meet deadlines measures time management. Actuals versus budgets measures cost control. Random sampling measures quality control.

In setting performance standards for operations, managers look at eight items:

1) Effectiveness;

2) Efficiency;

3) Company-wide (or total) quality;

4) Productivity;

5) Customer satisfaction;

6) Quality of work life;

7) Innovation; and

8) Financial performance.

To an operations person, the fundamental objective of making money translates into production, inventory and operational expense. Making money means keeping production high and inventory and expenses low.

A long tradition buttresses this thinking, but in fact, these days most managers with responsibility for operations spend their time doing three things—administering production, responding to crises and improving performance. Put another way, this means doing the job, putting out fires and adding new value.

Experience suggests that we spend most of our time doing the first two and not enough time doing the third. But we must do all three, and in the process, manipulate lots of information. We must data-detail what happens during the production cycle, and why.

The Payoff

The just-in-time inventory control system popularized by Japanese manufacturers shows how this information can pay off. In traditional manufacturing, someone delivers a big load of, say, car bumpers to the people on the production line who install them—more bumpers than the workers need for the day's output. So most sit on racks off to one side, waiting to be used.

The thinking here is that the company gains something by making one delivery of many bumpers. It does not consider the other side of the equation—namely the cost of a fat inventory. It does not measure the benefit of the single delivery of bumpers against the cost of loading up with more of them than necessary.

The Japanese made that measurement, inventing just-in-time inventory control and saving themselves a good deal of money. And they did it by measuring—by gathering information about the production process and asking what it meant. American managers followed suit, though it took them a while to overcome the biases of their traditional methods. By way of example, one management consultant tells of working as a summer intern at an appliance manufacturing plant in the Midwest. Detecting some inefficiencies in the plant's painting methods, he implemented a simple quality-control standard. He gathered data on the number of appliances that passed paint inspection and plotted a defect rate chart that he posted on a bulletin board.

Workers had never seen their defect rate graphed before and showed some interest in the charts. Their defect rate dropped from about 30 percent to about 5 percent.

Unfortunately, the story doesn't end here. After several weeks of improved performance, an upset operations supervisor tracked down the intern and asked about the charts. The intern, expecting praise, instead endured a hot lecture about the problems he had caused down the line. Because the defect rate in the painting operation had dropped so dramatically, the company had to lay off the people it hired just to fix the products with errors. And these people had nothing to do with the initial problem.

He told the intern to take his charts off the bulletin board.

Clearly, information generates improvements, but not without cost. The intern's charts threatened the jobs of the people down the line—a bad outcome to the angry supervisor who castigated the intern.

But that doesn't mean that you choose not to act on the information you gather. Critical thinking remains a management duty. So does innovation of the sort required to overcome the resistance to change personified by the painting supervisor in this story.

The Corporate Culture

Minnesota-based Zytec Corp. stakes its fortunes on gathering and using information about the production system. The company designs and manufactures power supplies for computers, medical gear, work stations—almost anything electronic. It posts annual revenues of $100 million and employs 900 people. It came out of a management-led buyout of a Control Data Corp. subsidiary in 1984.

At the time, management committed to using *hoshin kanri*. Literally translated from Japanese, *hoshin kanri* means controling the company's directional compass using methods of logic. It is generally defined as a discipline of policy deployment that includes all elements of a company in the planning process and relies heavily on information.

John Rogers, vice president of finance, says *hoshin kanri* "doesn't really address what most people call strategic planning. We start out in the early part of any given year with a series of meetings at our senior staff and board levels to [address] major issues—things that should be included. A lot of what the outside world calls strategic planning is done ad hoc by senior staff."

In preparing for the year ahead, the company develops separate plans for technical, marketing, manufacturing, materials and corporate functions put together by interdisciplinary groups consisting of 70 percent of experts in a given area and 30 percent of workers from other areas. The marketing group, for example, includes marketing staffers plus one engineer, one person from manufacturing and one from finance. Continuous improvement gets a high priority in formulating the plans; and the groups must come up with benchmarks to track improvement.

Four Objectives

Once done, the plans go to the people who implement them. Managers calculate the financial costs and benefits, and then a final version goes to the board of directors for approval. Senior managers compare the plans in order to coordinate their objectives. For 1994, Zytec's four objectives were to improve quality, improve the production cycle time, improve customer service and reduce costs.

The *hoshin kanri* system comes into play in the way it implements simple goals. "In a manufacturing team [where 12 to 15 people work as a cell on the manufacturing floor], one person will have attended a recent long range planning meeting [on benchmarks]," Rogers says. That person must communicate the objectives to the team—for example, to improve quality defined by faults per million—and how to go about it.

Team leaders review performance against objectives with senior staff once a month. The meetings, usually brief, present several graphs or other illustrations of the team's benchmarks. Managers say quickly what benchmarks have and have not been met. Staff then asks what resources the team needs to meet benchmarks.

Many team managers ask their entire teams to come to the meetings. Zytec has a total of 45 teams reporting monthly. So a senior manager hears 45 reports every month.

As for the payoff, Rogers offers an example: "We are committed to reducing cycle time necessary to produce basic documents—accounts payable checks and payroll checks," he says. "Since 1984, we slowly reduced time to about 10 percent of 1984 levels. [At that time,] something like 12 to 16 clerical people worked in accounting. Now we're substantially bigger than we were then and we have only three people there."

The system eats up the time of the people involved, but Zytec doesn't measure that cost. "It's part of our culture," Rogers says. "We don't evaluate in dollar sense; we evaluate in whether we can afford the time."

Zytec doesn't calculate the return on investment (ROI) generated by the *hoshin kanri* system, either. Asked to hazard a guess, Rogers says the system might use 2,000 man hours in a year. An average salary of $30,000 would bring the tab to $30,000, plus another $5,000 in other costs. "There's no question we get $35,000 of value out of it," he says. He dismisses ROI as speculative. Instead, Rogers argues, the *hoshin kanri* system supports Zytec's vision statement in a way no other system could.

The vision statement sets high standards:

> *Zytec is a company that competes on value; is market driven; provides superior quality and service; builds strong relationships with its customers; and provides technical excellence in its products.*

In 1998, Zytec merged with a long-time rival. Together they capture about 20 percent of the market. The expectation is that overhead will decline by 5 percent and that centralized procurement will result in a 10 percent reduction in the cost of materials.

Controling Inventory

Inventory makes a big target when operations sets out to improve your company's efficiency, but it presents managers with some hard questions.

"It's good to think of inventory as a liquid force," says one New York-based consultant. "It pours around the decisions you make about your business. You can't make hard policies about how your inventory will be. The best you can do is have a few priorities and use inventory as a kind of ongoing barometer of what's going on in your business."

With service companies, inventory includes the people available to work with clients. The drive for efficiency leads managers to embrace nontraditional employment and compensation structures—part-time or contract workers, and flexible teams operating as so-called "virtual corporations."

With manufacturing companies, some studies argue that you can reduce operating costs by more than 25 percent by managing inventory well. Things on shelves tie up cash; you spend money to make and maintain them—and then face the risk of damage or loss. Managers keep inventory as low as they can, at the risk of revenue-killing backlogs, spikes in supply costs and production scheduling nightmares.

Losers Accumulate

Things on shelves also test the effectiveness of your marketing efforts. A quick walk through your warehouse, for example, tells you a lot. Losers accumulate, winners disappear; products that don't sell take up storage space that could go to faster movers. If your shelves groan under products that you expected to sell, ask your sales force and marketers why.

Don't stockpile losers passively—which means don't ignore your inventory mix. You can cut inventory by 50 percent and still have piles of things in your warehouse that no one wants—a permanent and expensive inventory.

Some inventory problems have to do with the mix of products you stock, not with quantities. Retailers learn this the hard way. They balance the need to stay in stock against the need to turn inventory—a crucial measure of success in retailing. Most try to hit annual sales between 12 and 20 times inventory, which puts pressure on managers to keep only the best products in stock. A big mix of products worsens their problems by lowering storage capacity for any single product. And retailers must remain open to buy—that is, ready to purchase and stock hot items.

Managers in other businesses keep themselves open to buy by remaining flexible and market responsive even when it means taking less of a profit than you want out of one item, so as to free up money and space for another.

Growth also makes for complications in inventory control. You can't grow faster than you can deliver product to your customers. You may have to replenish inventory more often or stock more units of fewer products.

It's hard to quantify the connection, but some managers see inventory numbers as a reflection of accounts payable and receivable. Government contractors, for example, wait 60 days for payment, sometimes 90 days, and their accounts receivable run a deep negative. As a result, they rarely keep inventories larger than the value of their receivables minus payables.

"You need to figure out where all the money has to go to make the business function and know what the timing has to be," says a Maryland-based consultant to government contractors. "If you're fronting a lot of money to payroll and product development, you're not [going to have much left for carrying] a big inventory. Make sure you can absorb the growth until it is paid for."

Quality Control

Operations also governs quality control—and struggles more with this facet than with inventory control.

The goal of quality control is to make sure that the things you produce work as you promise they will. Good quality control makes for efficient operations by reducing the waste that goes with shoddy workmanship; quality control prevents the production of defective items you can't sell. But there are no rules of thumb here. You can't expect to wring 25 percent out of your production costs with good quality control, as you can with good inventory control. But you can measure it—and benefit from it.

A popular accounting tool for measuring quality is first-run yield (FRY) analysis. The concept starts out simply enough: if you inspect 100 products and find that 99 meet your quality specifications, the FRY rate for that product is 99 percent.

But it gets complicated. Each step in the process of making, storing and distributing product poses a new hazard to your FRY rate. If your manufacturing path entails many processes, the total FRY becomes the multiple of the FRYs of each process. In other words, the overall FRY for a process is the FRY of step A multiplied by the FRY of step B multiplied by the FRY of step C, etc.,—making a chain only as strong as its weakest link. If one process in your manufacturing chain posts a 50 percent FRY, the best FRY your company can show is 50 percent.

According to a Coopers & Lybrand study, the FRY rate averages 40 percent for companies in North America—a shocking number and a challenge to quality control.

The Answers

There are solutions to quality control problems. One, called operational strategic planning (OSP), essentially analyzes the facilities you use to make things and the ways in which you manage your use of those facilities. OSP seeks to bring about continuous quality improvement by studying your:

- Process and equipment needs;
- Computer and automation methods, maintenance and specifications;
- Systems design and control;
- Facilities design;
- Assembly operations;
- Quality assurance and inspection; and
- Production and inventory control.

OSP studies size, capacity, location, condition, specialization or focus, material handling and storage space utilization. It calculates the operating cost for each facility, compared to others within the same company or in the same industry sector.

This information in hand, OSP analyzes how management maximizes its use—or doesn't. It evaluates management information and control, design and manufacturing systems and quality systems. It also looks at peripheral influences such as your accounting and EDP systems, since they supply management with information to measure operations performance.

Defining the Problem

The OSP review then compares the use of technical and managerial assets. It defines problems by illustrating the difference between the two by asking questions such as:

- Can the company's hardware and software provide accurate, timely, meaningful information in a format that management can access easily?

- Does management understand and have confidence in the information provided by the systems?

- Has management used this information to improve production performance?

- Does the organization use human resources correctly and value these resources accurately? Does it have mechanisms in place to project payroll costs (including benefits and insurance costs like workers' comp)?

- Are facilities capable of being modified to design, make and store a changing product mix?

The answers to these questions should show you how to change and improve your operations strategy. Equipment and process capacity may increase or decrease but the capability and control will usually need improvement.

Your manufacturing processes will change if you shift to a more or less vertical integration, or to more outsourcing.

Group technology and just-in-time inventory may allow new plants to be smaller, while producing the same volume as older plants.

Changes in product technology may allow for a reduction of plant size or more production from the same plant.

Management information, control, design and manufacturing systems may need to be more sophisticated if tied to CAD/CAM and other computerized tools.

Last but not least, you may need fewer but more highly-trained personnel.

OSP consultants argue that you should identify all changes and include them in a pro forma operating budget, to establish whether you can meet performance requirements.

Another quality management tool that many managers favor is called just-in-time manufacturing. This technique emphasizes the elimination of waste, defined as anything beyond the minimum equipment, materials, space and labor needed to add value to the product or service. Just-in-time manufacturing draws heavily from inventory control applications and one from the next item on our list: Total Quality Management.

Total Quality Management

The inventor of Total Quality Management, W. Edwards Deming, began preaching his gospel of quality in Japan, where he went after World War II to help conduct a census. He had helped devise sampling techniques first used in the 1940 U.S. census, and in Japan, Deming lectured to top business leaders on statistical quality control. He told the businessmen that Japan could dominate world markets if it stressed his definition of quality in its manufacturing operations.

Deming identified three phases of change that companies go through on the road to improved performance measurement systems:

1) Tinkering with the existing measurement system (e.g. the cost accounting system);

2) Cutting the knot between accounting and performance measurement; and

3) Embracing change in strategies, actions and measures.

Deming believed in on-line quality control rather than end-line control. To achieve this, analysts sample products during manufacturing in order to determine the product's deviation from an accepted range of errors. As Deming saw it, any deviation is the result of one of two kinds of variables, either a special cause stemming from random events or a common cause arising from faults in the system. Deming argued that special causes account for only 6 percent of all variations and common causes for 94 percent. (He also liked to say that bad management caused 85 percent of the quality and productivity problems in business.) In his view, most companies spend too much time trying to determine the nature of special causes rather than examining the system to find out what's behind the common causes.

Deming's analysis relies heavily on mathematics—a product of his background as a government statistician. "People who are more number-oriented are more likely to use a Deming approach," says Massachusetts management consultant Michael Galardi.

But you don't have to be Stephen Hawking to understand Deming. He believed quality improves as variability decreases—a simple idea. To monitor variance, he advocated a statistical method of quality control. He argued that companies should strive for continuous improvement using statistical methods and analysis to maintain quality, instead of inspecting products en masse for defects once they have been manufactured.

Deming's work remained theoretical, but his many students have assembled a body of literature and consulting advice that gives the concepts a practical spin.

Growth and Quality

California-based Sunrise Medical Inc. makes wheelchairs, hospital beds and patient aids that ease the lives of the disabled and the elderly. With revenues now over $600 million a year, Sunrise doesn't count as a small company, but founder Richard Chandler ran the company like a bootstrap operation. He cut costs, insisted on improving quality and invested heavily in product development.

Chandler started Sunrise in 1983 with $4.5 million in seed capital raised primarily from venture capital firms. His idea came out of the fact that the growing number of elderly people and an active disabled population would increase the demand for high-quality medical products.

Sunrise had an early success with its Quickie Wheelchair division, which makes custom-built chairs designed for an individual's height, weight and color preferences. Quickie has become the country's leading maker of lightweight manual wheelchairs. The division's sales have grown some 20 percent a year since 1987 and account for more than a third of Sunrise's total revenues. Managed care has continually pushed the company toward lower cost approaches.

Nevertheless, Chandler felt something was missing from his corporate game plan. Neither product quality nor employee motivation were as high as he wanted them to be. "People don't want to work to improve earnings per share. That doesn't turn anybody on," he told one newspaper. "You have to define a greater purpose."

That purpose came to him during a 1987 trip to Japan. After touring Toyota and Matsushita operations, Chandler realized that Sunrise—despite its success—wasn't realizing its potential in terms of quality control.

He decided to remake Sunrise in three ways: by revamping his manufacturing operations, revamping his research program and by improving his worker loyalty.

With respect to manufacturing, Sunrise adopted just-in-time manufacturing principles. This meant keeping a thin inventory—only material needed for producing and shipping products within 24 hours. The smaller inventories saved the company $20 million in the first four years. In addition, workers organized into self-directed teams. When a production problem arose, teams had the authority to take any actions necessary to solve it. This cut production down-time and improved employee motivation.

Product Innovation

With respect to research, Chandler decided to plow almost all profits back into product innovation. Between 1987 and 1993, research spending more than doubled to $4.21 million, or 2 percent of revenues, a year. (The company's long-term goal: R&D spending of 4 percent of revenues.) The research allowed Sunrise to use advanced metals and plastics in wheelchairs, reducing chair weights almost in half. By spending $600,000 to develop an all-plastic bedside toilet chair, Sunrise created a rust-proof product 20 percent less expensive than standard metal chairs.

With respect to worker loyalty, Sunrise developed an incentive program that rewards outstanding efforts. Most of Sunrise's workers weren't highly paid; wages at one plant averaged less than $10 an hour. To convince workers at that level to support a quality program, the company made its basic, company-wide goals known to all workers and celebrated achievement of specific ones.

The payoff: with improving quality and productivity numbers, Sunrise started an international expansion in the early 1990s. It made several strategic acquisitions in Europe and other markets. Its products sell in some 60 countries; international sales have grown at an average rate of around 30 percent annually for the past 10 years.

Although Sunrise ran into some financial problems in the mid-1990s, it is now bouncing back. It launched the industry's first on-line ordering system in 1999, both for its authorized supplier and consumers, offering its full product line of over 7,000 individual items.

Deming's disciples identify 10 elements of total quality management. His statistical control theories may not apply to your operations, but you can use these points as a kind of diagnostic checklist.

On a day-to-day basis, do you emphasize:

1. **Customer-orientation.** Methods, processes and procedures are designed to meet both internal and external customer expectations.

2. **Leadership.** Top management understands the quality process and supports the strategy through both words and deeds.

3. **Full employee participation.** Everyone in the organization is provided quality training. From top to bottom, everyone has the perspective, goals and necessary tools and techniques for improving quality.

4. **A sensible reward system.** There is a system in place that rewards quality to ensure continuous support for the overall effort.

5. **Reduced cycle time.** There is a strong effort to reduce the cycle times, in product or service output as well as support functions, following the maxim: "If it cannot be done any better, focus on doing it faster."

6. **Prevention, not detection.** Quality is designed into the product or service, so that errors are prevented rather than detected and subsequently corrected.

7. **Management by fact.** Managers use data-based feedback to measure progress; intuition and gut feeling are put on the back burner.

8. **Long-range outlook.** There is a constant monitoring of the external environment in order to answer the question: What level of quality or service must we provide to customers over the next 12 to 36 months, and how can this goal be attained?

9. **Partnership development.** The organization promotes cooperation with vendors as well as customers, thus developing a network system that helps drive up quality and hold down costs.

10. **Public responsibility.** Corporate citizenship and responsibility are fostered by sharing quality-related information with other organizations, and by working to reduce negative impacts on the community by eliminating product waste generation, product defects or recalls.

All of these characteristics apply to running a business in general. The fifth, sixth and ninth apply directly to operations.

More recently, Genichi Taguchi, another total quality consultant, has gained influence among managers with complex production and operations functions. Taguchi built his reputation as the head of research at the Electrical Communications Laboratory of Nippon Telephone and Telegraph. In 1960, he received Japan's Deming Award for his work applying quality management at a huge corporate institution.

"Quality is a virtue of design," Taguchi writes. "The robustness of products is more a function of good design than on-line control, however stringent, of manufacturing processes."

Taguchi argues that managers concentrating on the goal of zero defects have grown accustomed to viewing quality in terms of acceptable deviations from a target—rather than the effort to hit the target. The more a company deviates from targets, he contends, the bigger its losses. Taguchi quantifies this loss in a mathematical formula known as the Quality Loss Function. QLF provides an effective technique to measure the cost to the customer of product defects.

Success in the Real World

Pennsylvania-based New Standard Corp., a machine toolmaker, has applied progressive management strategies to a traditional heavy-industry operation. Chairman and CEO Morton Zifferer gained notice because of his commitment to management philosophies more commonly found in high-tech, not low-tech, industry.

Indeed, New Standard's plants look like industrial America from an earlier time. Its operations include almost 100 presses with rated capacities from five tons to 2,700 tons and specialized machines that assemble everything from high-speed impeller assemblies to parts for hedge trimmers.

But New Standard's performance would make any modern manufacturer happy. The company has reported steady growth for more than 10 years.

Revenues have reached over $30 million annually since the mid-1990s, up from less than $10 million 10 years previously. Its 300 associates manufacture parts for a client list that includes Black & Decker, Caterpillar, Mack Truck and Westinghouse.

The company started out as a lawn and garden tool manufacturer in the early 1900s. Zifferer's father turned it into a repeat-order manufacturing facility. Morton Zifferer bought out his sisters in 1984 and began buying out his father in 1991.

Zifferer's business cards carry New Standard's mission statement:

> *To continuously improve our safe, secure, high integrity, team-based organization, through which we engineer and manufacture metal products that exceed our customers' expectations, assuring profitable long-term associations, while improving the quality of our lives.*

New Standard's vision statement asserts that the company seeks to become "a cellular organizational structure that stimulates teamwork at all levels...and foster a company-wide culture that stresses continuous improvement of every process for every customer."

A Commitment

"The real opportunity is that people understand that continuous improvement is forever," Zifferer says. "We have an incredible commitment to education. All salary adjustments will be on a pay-for-skills basis."

Indeed, some company employees spend as much as 15 percent of their work day involved in some form of education, either in matters specific to their jobs or of a more general nature. "In true systems, everyone shares," Zifferer says. "You give smart people the opportunity to be empowered, testing their willingness to accept responsibility."

Zifferer's father taught him that being bigger wasn't better. "Being *best* is," he says. Furthermore, he translates this notion into reality by practicing what he calls agile manufacturing.

"In agile manufacturing," he adds, "you can anticipate what it is that your customer may not even know he wants."

New Standard stands apart because it has accomplished so much under Zifferer's watch. In 1993, the company added four new presses to the larger of its two plants and redesigned the smaller one to focus on "advance value engineering."

In 1989, Zifferer invited Ryuji Fukuda, an internationally reputed productivity expert, for a week-long seminar on improving quality. Fukuda, who has worked with Sony and Sumitomo, earned a Deming prize in the 1970s for his work on continuous quality improvement.

Zifferer boasts that New Standard has worked closely on new product development projects with Black & Decker. "We worked with them from pretty crude designs through the stampings, without any blueprints," he told one local newspaper. "Other things we're looking for in the future are manufacturability and assembly but also reassembly and disassembly to replace pieces."

Zifferer says that by applying the quality control theories of people like Deming and Fukuda, his coworkers achieve high accuracy rates with traditional tools. This makes 50-year-old cutting tools capable of laser-like accuracy.

"The benchmark of quality [is] the number of defects per million," says Zifferer. "Twenty per million is very acceptable. It's a good benchmark, but once you get there, you've got to get to the next level."

The Bottom Line

Operations is the most deductive of business functions. Its objectives can be defined very clearly against predictable standards of performance and cost control.

But operations doesn't manage itself; you can't ignore operations or delegate management to junior people. On the contrary, many managers begin their efforts at overall improvement with operations because they see the most money to be saved and the greatest improvement to product quality.

In operations as in financial matters, you can bring about a substantial improvement by using a series of basic analytic tools. Look for areas where you can improve your operations.

Ask Yourself:

- [ ] Do you do self-audits on your own records and the maintenance of equipment?

- [ ] Do you have back-up suppliers for most of your manufacturing process needs?

- [ ] Do you have adequate internal quality controls or are your customers the first to know if one of your processes failed?

- [ ] Are your facilities that are adequate for today also adequate for your growth plans?

- [ ] Do you have a working just-in-time inventory system?

- [ ] Are your facilities and information systems prepared for a natural disaster or other physically destructive force?

- [ ] Are you making the best use of available new technologies in manufacturing?

- [ ] Are you tailoring new operations strategies for use on the Internet or for sales via e-commerce?

- [ ] Do you regularly chart and review operational performance?

Unit Output by Product

This worksheet gives you a method to monitor production output by product for each month, year to date and on average.

You can use this worksheet to compare how many units you produce each month with how many units you sell of each product. It also allows you to see what products have increased your production, and what products have decreased your production (presumably due to increases or decreases in sales).

If output exceeds sales by a wide margin, you are increasing your inventory. If sales exceed output, you are using up inventory and running the risk of backorders over time.

The main benefit of doing this analysis is to post the numbers. This lets people know someone is paying attention to what they are doing. There is also the natural tendency of people to want to outdo themselves. Posting these numbers allows people to see their progress in increasing productivity.

List each product you manufacture and, at the end of each month, enter the number of units produced. Keep a running tally of total year-to-date output in the first shaded column.

Enter the average for the year in the last column.

Do this three times: once for last year, once to make projections for the current year, and once over the course of the year with actual numbers month to month.

Lastly, enter the output numbers for the prior year at the bottom of the page.

Ask Yourself:

- ☐ Is output on the rise for all products?

- ☐ Does output approximately match sales numbers?

- ☐ Is output up over last year?

- ☐ Are any of the trends indicative of factors that might affect production cycles in the coming year?

- ☐ How do unit-output figures compare with unit-revenue figures? In other words, what are your most cost-effective products?

Go to worksheet on the following page   →

Business Plans to Game Plans

Unit Output By Product   ☐ Actuals last year

PRODUCT	1 Jan.	2 Feb.	3 Mar.	4 April	5 May	6 June
Totals						

Unit Output last year

Jan.	Feb.	Mar.	April	May	June

☐ **Projections for this year**   ☐ **Actuals for this year**

7 July	8 Aug.	9 Sept.	10 Oct.	11 Nov.	12 Dec.	Unit Output Year-to-date	Avg. Unit Output by Mo.[1]

[1]Divide total year-to-date unit sales by current month number.

July	Aug.	Sept.	Oct.	Nov.	Dec.

Units Shipped

This worksheet tracks the number of products shipped each week and each month.

Another way to get a feel for sales each month is to know how many units were shipped. Regardless of the variety of prices charged for different products, generally speaking, if units shipped are up, sales probably are too.

Units shipped is also a good gauge for determining whether to hire new production and fulfillment personnel. After using this form for a period of time, it is possible to determine how many units an average person can ship. If your totals get over this number, you may need to hire temporary help, or even hire regular help for an ongoing need.

List your products in the left-hand column. Track the number of units shipped each day for each of your products and enter the number once a week.

At the end of the month, total the columns for each week in the total shipped column. Divide this total by four or five to determine the average number of units shipped per week. Enter this number in the last column.

At the bottom of the worksheet, list units shipped in total for each month of the current year and the previous year.

Ask Yourself:

☐ Are total units shipped up over last year?

☐ Is there a seasonality to your sales that means you have more units to be shipped at certain times of the year?

☐ How much of your weekly and/or monthly shipments were backorders? What's your current backlog?

☐ How do spikes in the Units Shipped figures alter your inventory control systems? Can you absorb some fluctuation? How much?

☐ Do these numbers seem to track with expectations based on sales figures for the same period of time?

Go to worksheet on the following page ➔

Units Shipped for _____
(month/year)

Product	Week 1	Week 2	Week 3
Totals			

Items shipped this year

Jan.	Feb.	Mar.	April	May	June	July

Items shipped last year

Jan.	Feb.	Mar.	April	May	June	July

Week 4	Week 5	Total shipped	Average Units shipped per week

Aug.	Sept.	Oct.	Nov.	Dec.

Aug.	Sept.	Oct.	Nov.	Dec.

Average Days to Ship

This worksheet helps you determine how long your customers have to wait between the time they place an order and the time the product is sent to them.

This worksheet will be most useful if you set a standard to meet. Use the average number of days to ship as a tracking for a service standard that you want to meet or beat.

Many companies try to ship off-the-shelf products within 24 or 48 hours of the order.

Identify your orders (usually by order number) in column one. For each order, enter the date the order was placed by the customer. In the third column, enter the date the order was actually shipped. Enter the number of days' difference between the order date and the date shipped in the last column.

At the bottom of the worksheet, take the total number of days from the shaded box at the bottom right and divide by the number of orders you have listed in the first column. This number is the number of days, on average, between the time the customer placed the order and the time it is shipped out to them.

Ask Yourself:

☐ Is your current average number of days to ship an acceptable number to you? What is standard in your industry?

☐ What can your company do to decrease that number?

☐ Does seasonality or any other external factor influence turn-around time? If so, what can you do to anticipate this?

☐ Can you make a short turnaround time a stated goal for your company? Can you do this effectively?

☐ Again, how do these figure affect your inventory control?

Average Days To Ship

_____
(month/year)

Order #	Order Date	Order Shipped	Days From Order To Ship
1.			
2.			
3.			
4.			
5.			
6.			
7.			
8.			
9.			
10.			
11.			
12.			
13.			
14.			
15.			
16.			
17.			
18.			
19.			
20.			
21.			
22.			
23.			
24.			
25.			

$$\frac{\text{TOTAL days from order to ship}}{\text{TOTAL \# of orders}} = \boxed{\qquad\qquad} \text{ Average days to ship}$$

- [ ] At what point does the time it takes you to ship an order start to interfere with sales?

- [ ] To what extent do different products require different turn-around times? Can you segregate shipping functions to handle these variations more efficiently?

Returns Analysis

This worksheet helps you determine how many of the units you send to customers are returned to you, and why they are returned. It's a diagnostic tool.

As with many other worksheets in this section, it is important to track measures of productivity. If employees know you are paying attention to this measure, they will seek to improve the statistics themselves over time.

List your products in the far left column. Then list the total quantity returned for each product in the second column. The third column is broken into 10 separate sections. Each section has a reason for return code number that is explained to the right.

Enter the total quantity returned for each reason in this section. At the bottom of the columns, enter the total numbers for reasons 1-6 and reasons 7-10.

Reasons for return numbers 1 through 6 are errors on the part of the company. Use this worksheet to track these numbers, set goals and decrease them over time.

At the bottom left of the worksheet, enter the total units shipped. Calculate the percentage of shipments returned by dividing the total returns in the first shaded box by the total number of units shipped. Calculate the percentage of shipments returned for reasons 1-6 by dividing the second shaded box by the total number of units shipped.

In the area at the bottom of the worksheet, enter the number of shipments returned for reasons 1-6 for each month this year and last year.

Returns Analysis

for _____
(month/year)

Returns By Product:

Product	Total Quantity Returned	Quantity Returned By Reason*									
		1	2	3	4	5	6	7	8	9	10
Total Returns		**Total reasons 1-6**						**Total reasons 7-10**			

Percentage of shipments returned for reasons 1 - 6:

This year:

Jan.	Feb.	Mar.	April	May	June	July	Aug.	Sept.	Oct.	Nov.	Dec.

This month last year:

Jan.	Feb.	Mar.	April	May	June	July	Aug.	Sept.	Oct.	Nov.	Dec.

From *Units Shipped* worksheet:

TOTAL UNITS SHIPPED

% of shipments returned

% of shipments returned for reasons 1 - 6

*RETURN CODES
1. Product not ordered
2. Shipment received damaged
3. Wrong product received/ order entry error
4. Wrong product received/ shipping error
5. Product defective
6. Quality not as expected
7. Overstock
8. Customer changed mind
9. Exchange (old editions for new)
10. Other/don't know

273

Ask Yourself:

- [ ] Overall, are your returns increasing or decreasing?

- [ ] Is there any meaningful link between types of product and number of returns? Does this suggest anything for marketing or product development projects?

- [ ] Are many of the returns caused by problems on your end (reasons 1 through 6), or are they mostly due to customer needs changes?

- [ ] Do you think the number of returns could be lowered? If so, how?

- [ ] Would returns be lower if customers better understood your product at the time they ordered?

Backlog of Orders

This worksheet helps you determine whether any orders have not been shipped by the end of the week (or other period of time that you choose).

This is very important as a diagnostic monitor of production bottlenecks. A backlog occurs when an order is not shipped. This could be for a variety of reasons: the product may not be available, packaging may not be available or shipping may be too busy to get it out.

Any items on this list should be investigated. The dollar volume column that is totaled on the bottom of the sheet will really focus your attention. Like excess inventory, backlog orders sap a company's productivity.

Knowing this report will have to be made each week will usually prompt the shipping department to get all the orders out that it can.

This worksheet should be filled in by shipping or customer service personnel every Friday. Any orders not shipped by the end of the week should be documented by order number and customer name.

Also entered should be the dollar volume of the order, and the date the order was placed. The expected ship date and comments should indicate why the order was not shipped, and when it will be shipped.

Week of _____

Backlog of Orders

Order #	Customer	$ Volume of Order	Order Date	Expected Ship Date	Comments

TOTAL

The total dollar volume of all the orders not shipped should be entered at the bottom of the worksheet.

Ask Yourself:

☐ Are there orders backlogged every week or only occasionally?

☐ Are the reasons for backlogs usually the same?

☐ Are these problems that can be corrected? If so, how?

☐ How many of these orders will be canceled due to product unavailability?

☐ Has this problem gotten worse over time? With the same products?

Top 10 Critical Suppliers Log

This worksheet tracks what suppliers your company spends the most money with each year and determines how much money you spend.

It is interesting to see with whom your company spends the most money each year. You may be on the list of this suppliers' most important customers and represent a relationship they would like to expand. Take advantage of this condition.

You can—like some aggressive managers—tell suppliers that you know you spent $20,000 (or more) with them in the past year and that they might get more of your business if they're willing to negotiate on price discounts and/or terms.

It is also a good practice to look at what you are spending with any given supplier for a whole year. We often don't realize what we spend in total when we receive monthly invoices.

Taking a look at top suppliers also helped my company set limits for how much we wanted to spend in particular categories.

The log also helps to spot trends where over-reliance on one supplier or source could be risky if they cannot perform.

List all of the regular suppliers you send checks to each year and rank order them by top dollar volume down. Enter them by name and the product or service they provide in the first two columns. Last, enter the dollar volume you have spent with them this year. You may also want to do this exercise for the last full year and see if your spending with these suppliers has gone up or down.

Ask Yourself:

☐ Are these services that you spend so much on each year critical to the profitability of the company?

☐ Can you bid these services out to explore whether you're getting the most value for your dollars spent?

☐ Can you talk with any of these vendors about fee reductions for a certain dollar volume of business?

☐ Do these expenditures suggest weaknesses or strengths in your management structure?

☐ Are you reliant on only one supplier for a critical element of your business? Do you have back-up plans in case that supplier goes out of business or is otherwise unable to supply what you need?

☐ If you have done business with the same supplier for three years or more, are you certain that they still produce the best value or the most state of the art product?

Top 10 Vendors — Critical Supplier Log
(Ranked by $ Volume)

Name	Product or Service
1.	
2.	
3.	
4.	
5.	
6.	
7.	
8.	
9.	
10.	

$ Volume spent with them this year

Inventory Control Report

This worksheet helps you determine your total inventory over a set time period and where your inventory is inadequate to meet sales needs.

This is another very important indicator of production bottlenecks.

Any items listed at the bottom of the page should be questioned. Asking the right questions at this stage could prevent these products from showing up on the backlog list later.

Enter the total inventory numbers from the year at a glance financial analysis worksheet for each month this year and last year.

In the three column chart, list all products with less that two months' inventory at current sales levels, list quantity currently on hand and note when restocking is expected.

This worksheet is an essential step in any move toward a just-in-time inventory management system.

Ask Yourself:

☐ Is total inventory going up or down?

☐ Does inventory fluctuate in a cyclical or seasonal pattern? If so, can you use these patterns to manage inventory in the future?

☐ Does this increase or decrease fit with your cash management strategies?

☐ Will your restocking dates allow you to replenish your inventory supply before you run out of product?

☐ What do inventory fluctuations suggest about your market sector? Your customers? Your internal operations?

Inventory Control Report
for _____
(month/year)

Total Inventory

This month:

Jan. Feb. Mar. April May June July Aug. Sept. Oct. Nov. Dec.

This month last year:

Jan. Feb. Mar. April May June July Aug. Sept. Oct. Nov. Dec.

Inventory at Low Level:

List below any items with under two months inventory on hand.

Product Description	Quantity Currently on hand	Expected Restock Date

Business Partner (Supplier) Survey

This survey assesses how your suppliers feel about their relationship with your company. Using this data to improve your business relationships may lead to lowering your costs as well.

Be sure and send this form to your Top Ten Critical Suppliers and preferably to at least 20 others.

You may only get back a small percentage of surveys sent. You can increase this response rate if you call ahead and tell your supplier contact to expect it, or if you send the survey with an order. Try to give them a deadline for its return. The larger the number returned, the better the data you have from which to draw conclusions. You might consider asking the form to be returned directly to the company president by including a self-addressed, stamped envelope. You will get a better response and the responses will be more meaningful if suppliers believe their survey comments will be read by the president of the company.

Tabulate response by taking each question individually, totaling the 1-10 score received, and dividing that number by the number of surveys received with that question answered. This will give you an average score for each question.

Distribute your scores throughout the company. Congratulate yourself on scores of 8-10. Continue to improve on scores of 5-7. Consider scores of 4 or under to require immediate attention focused on those area of your company. Put together interdepartmental task forces to devise action plans to increase your levels of service.

Particularly consider the remarks in the comments sections. Call any suppliers who requested one, and do so within a week of receiving their completed survey. Send a thank you note to all suppliers who filled in their name at the bottom of the survey.

This survey should be done annually and results trended over time.

Business Partner (Supplier) Survey

Questions	1-10	Comments
Do you enjoy doing business with us?		
Do you feel we treat you as a vendor or as a business partner?		
Do our employees treat you courteously?		
Are you paid on time?		
Are we a larger or a smaller customer? (10= largest)		
Do we supply you with enough information about our business for you to do your best work with us?		
Do we give you enough time to fill our orders?		

Could we make any changes in our business practices that would help us reduce your costs and result in lower prices for us?

How could our relationship with you change to benefit us both?

Are there other comments in areas we missed in this survey?

❑   There is more to say and I would like you to telephone me. Best time to call is

‾‾‾‾‾‾‾‾‾‾‾‾‾‾‾‾‾‾‾‾‾‾‾ .

Name and Company Name (optional)

Ask Yourself:

☐ Are you making it easy for suppliers to do business with your company?

☐ Are your employees creating partnerships with suppliers or treating them as vendors?

☐ What can you do to immediately change supplier perception for the better?

☐ Have suppliers told you anything that surprises you about the ethics of their communications with your employees?

☐ Are your scores trended up or down over time?

CHAPTER 8:

HUMAN RESOURCES

The management of the human resources in your company determines the success or failure of almost all of the other goals you have set for yourself. If you manage people well in all aspects—hiring, training, coaching, reviewing, compensating, motivating, promoting and celebrating—then the impossible often becomes possible.

Think of the difference one person can make when highly motivated to get something done. Then think of a group of people, working together toward a common goal. A quality team of people working together is your single biggest competitive advantage. Don't lose the game here. Don't assume that you pay them to come to work and that ought to be enough.

The single biggest mistake that CEOs and managers make is to spend more time analyzing and acting on the financial numbers than on the people issues in the company. There should be monthly management staff meetings to review the data you will compile with the worksheets in this section. Management performance should be reviewed by how well managers carry out the actions decided upon in these meetings.

Look at your payroll as an investment. It is just as important to have a plan for your human resource dollars as for any of the money you spend on plant and materials. Start-up Internet companies best illustrate this point. There are people and there is technology. Sometimes there isn't even an office or any inventory.

Quantity and Quality

As a beginning, you need to know both how many employees are optimal to do the work, and what skills and qualities you want them to have. You can look at the quantitative issues both objectively, by looking at overtime rates or temporary help needed and numbers of errors made, and subjectively, by the amount of stress you see in the workplace and what other employees tell you.

You may readily know the skills you think you need from new employees, but you can also do a more objective analysis by listing what total skill set you want from your employee base. Find out what you already have by doing a skill set inventory. Then hire for what you still find missing.

That is the easy part. What is much more difficult is listing the types of character traits you want your employees to possess. How important are initiative and resourcefulness? How about trustworthiness and loyalty? This analysis is more likely to prevent employee lawsuit headaches later than any other.

Hiring Right Is Key

Recruiting and hiring is usually done in haste, leaving the company to repent at leisure. An employee gives two weeks' notice or workload suddenly gets heavy and the hiring process becomes short shrift. To counteract this tendency, set up your hiring process at a time when more rational heads prevail, and make it difficult—if not impossible—to hire unless the process is completed. At a minimum you should:

Require some outside testing. Allow a competent, impartial professional interviewer to give both paper and verbal tests. I find that testing often validates suspicions about questionable people—and forces me to deal with potentially problematic employees.

Do a rigorous personal interview. This includes questions related to: general attitude, managing your boss, managing your staff, understanding the financial workings of a business and your department's part in the business's overall success, your ability to set goals and your own expectations about achieving goals, and the specific skills required for the job and general communications required by the job. Set up questions to be asked on a worksheet so that the interviewer can jot notes underneath each question during the interview.

I immediately disqualify anyone who has been dishonest about any information they have given and that is pertinent to the hiring decision. I suggest a statement on the application that information must be true and that it will be checked. Dishonest applicants need not apply. Yes, and that includes fudging on job titles, years of service and salary history.

Have peer group interviews. This part of the process allows the applicant to talk more freely and helps you evaluate how comfortably that person will work with his or her peers. Follow this up with a meeting of everyone involved in the hiring decision to see if there is a consensus among the group.

Do a background check. Don't neglect this task, even if it is an employee's cousin or your competitor's best sales person. It is very easy to set up an account with an investigative firm on-line and fairly quickly and cheaply find out if there is a criminal record, a DMV record of problems, a history of other lawsuits involving employers or a history of workers' comp problems, etc.

Do a reference check. This can be done by telephone but may require a request in writing. Although reference checking is less effective than it used to be, you may still find a few people willing to talk. Most former employers play it safe and only verify dates of employment and salary.

Corporate Culture

Karen Forys was named Washington State Superintendent of the Year in 1999. Karen believes in welcoming each new employee to her district by reminding them that the purpose of her schools—a devotion to student learning—hasn't changed for the past 100 years. She brings her new employee orientation to life by dressing in 1880s schoolteacher garb and talking about the one-room schoolhouse in which the first teacher in the district taught. She set benchmarks for success when she took the superintendent's job in 1993. Today, the dropout rate in her district is among the lowest in the state and her district ranks among the top in Washington in standardized test scores.

Corporate culture is not what you'd like people to think but rather, what it *feels* like to be at your company. An employee orientation that sets the stage is great. Trust is essential. You can run your company as an autocrat or as an active participant among employees—both can be successful. The key, however, is consistency. Don't tell them they have a say in a decision if they really don't. Don't feel pressured by the management gurus to take employee input on issues if you have already decided the way it is going to be. If you are not authentic, you will lose trust.

Another Overused Word: Feedback

Feedback is a management concept like empowerment: it's great to discuss in theory, but it's not often implemented with employees in a meaningful way.

Feedback means letting employees know how they are doing individually and how their department and the company as a whole is performing in all sorts of ways. Feedback is often subjective, but it can be objective as well. The best kind of feedback comes when an employee seeks out a response, and not when feedback is forced upon him. If your intranet has easily available sales data, sales employees will look at it often and judge their need to change performance accordingly. The best situation is to allow employees to change their behavior on their own or ask for help before they are officially evaluated.

Give employees copies of all of the evaluation materials that will be used during their employment (surveys, annual review forms, team feedback tools) at their orientation. They will know what is expected of them by knowing how they will be evaluated.

Effective Communication

Productive and positive communication with an immediate supervisor as well as other employees is a make-or-break issue for most employees. As we all know, in the world of work there is formal communication and informal communication. Formal communication generates from the supervisor and follows the policies and procedures in the manual. Informal communications come from other employees about "the way things are really done around here." The more out of balance these two sets of communications are, the lower the morale at your company.

Make your internal computer network a resource for every kind of data your employees need. Virtually all of the worksheets covered in this book can be filled with your company's information and made available for employee reference. Your employee handbook should also be made available on-line. Surveys can be done completely via e-mail. Make sure the CEO is accessible by e-mail for questions or comments, and that employees will get timely responses.

By no means should communication be done exclusively by computer. Always do employee orientations and performance reviews face to face. Create other avenues for informal, face-to-face feedback as well. Put them on your calendar so time won't slip by and opportunities won't be missed. Morning coffees, celebration lunches, afternoon walks or brown bag resource talks all add valuable opportunities for discussing issues and developing rapport.

Gauging Employee Opinions

On the more formal side, survey employees at least annually to see what they really think of their work environment. The only category where you generally hope to find mediocre ratings is in compensation. After all, do you expect to have employees tell you that they think their pay is just right or more than enough?

I also found it important to survey not only on employee comfort and culture, but also on company performance on much bigger issues, such as our ethical attitudes and socially responsible behaviors.

The Virginia-based AES Corporation is the largest global power company in the world. It was founded almost 20 years ago and now has well over 100 power plants in 16 countries. It also employees over 40,000 people around the world. Their Web site says the following:

> *AES recognizes that most companies have standards and ethics by which they operate and that business decisions are based, at least in part, by such principles. The Company believes that an explicit commitment to a particular set of standards is a useful way to encourage ownership of those values among its people. While the people at AES acknowledge that they won't always live up to these standards, they believe that being held accountable to these shared values will help them behave more consistently with such principles.*

AES believes that every employee should participate in the strategic planning process, and even in designing their own work places. It also has four declared principles: integrity, fairness, fun and social responsibility. AES believes in surveys. They annually survey employees at individual locations and throughout the company. Their surveys are written to determine whether their ethical principles are followed by their employees both with other employees and with customers and suppliers.

AES follows through with their principles into their organizational structure. They have no human resources department, but instead utilize self-managed work teams that handle these responsibilities for the respective employees.

Gauging Employee Performance

Performance reviews should be conducted annually, with quarterly mini-goal-checking sessions. Schedule these for times when you will be fresh and when your mind won't be elsewhere. Do them off-site if that's what it takes to be sure you aren't distracted. If you put a lot of thought into the process up front, then the employees will do most of the preparation for the sessions themselves.

It is important to ask employees to give feedback about what is standing in their way of progress as a prelude to a review session. Although many HR professionals advocate having employees formally rate themselves and then compare the managers' rating with their own in the formal session, I find this leads to a lot of anxiety and not a lot of dialogue. Usually if you ask someone what is holding him back and what you can do to help, he will candidly explore his own weaknesses and will be open to feedback.

During the review meeting, turn these areas for improvement into goals for the coming year. Ask the employee to consider ways to transform these weaknesses into goal statements with measurements by quarter. These automatically become subjects for your quarterly reviews.

More controversial is the idea of team performance reviews. Members of a peer group evaluate an employee, in addition to his or her supervisor review. While I see tremendous value in the concept, the average employee today is not ready to accept criticism from peers—she barely tolerates it from the supervisor. It creates anger and resentment rather than increased learning unless months of preparation precede this feedback. The best way to transition into this system is to make it available as a tool for self-evaluation to those individuals who seek promotions. If employees are open to learning about how they are perceived (because they themselves want to use this information to increase their opportunities), then they will most likely be better able to accept the negative messages.

I also believe managers should be reviewed on their managerial effectiveness. Employees also need to know that they will have the opportunity to speak candidly about their manager's behavior.

Make Time to Manage

Conduct regular monthly meetings devoted only to human resource issues. A tool that can be reviewed during each meeting is a simple employee ranking system. This helps the department manager judge each employee's overall performance for staff planning purposes. Use a simple 1-10 scale, ranking your superstars as 9s or 10s and regarding your 4s or below as employees who no longer belong in their current jobs or perhaps with your company. This categorization is done in a variety of dimensions for a composite score. The ranking is accomplished by character, communications skills, and lastly, technical abilities.

The intent of this process is not only to review employees, but to keep the manager accountable for constant improvement in the caliber of the personnel employed. What is the manager doing each month to create more 9s and 10s?

The Management Team

This brings us to the subject of the people who rank all the other people—your management staff. Managers, themselves, should all rank 8 and above, or be so new that you expect them to be at an 8 within six months. There is no way to get around this. Without 8s or above as managers, your company is not providing models for the rest of the staff. Most managers start out as highly skilled technical people who are promoted to overseeing a group. But these type of people are not always the best managers. A manager's key skill is coaching great performance out of others. And this is what a company should look for when promoting or hiring for managerial positions.

While a manager performs her daily tasks of recruiting, hiring, disciplining and terminating those who work for her, she must continually assess and improve the employee's knowledge, willingness and action on the job.

One of the most important characteristics of a superior workforce is that all employees stay employable. This means that you employ who your competitors would want to hire if they could. A goal of your human resource planning should be to have state of the art employees. And your employees should know what is expected of them; they probably will have to invest in themselves with outside training to keep their end of this bargain.

Destructive Employees

There are some things that just should not be tolerated in the work environment. They are toxic to your culture and will hurt your workplace immeasurably if not checked. While they may seem harmless in small doses, they are not.

Most managers make the mistake of keeping employees around long after they know they are not right for the job. We feel we want to give people a chance. Only give employees who have made mistakes a second chance. Employees whose actions reveal a lack of character and unethical behavior should not be allowed to continue destroying the company.

You may think judging employees' ethics is inappropriate—that they should be judged on work performance alone. Whether you know it or like it, you set ethical standards in many ways: your own behavior, the rules in your employee handbook, the performance review process, the compensation system and by how and who you promote. You set standards by what behavior you encourage and what behavior you tolerate in your employees.

A recent study done by two professors for Bell and Howell Information and Learning confirms that the behavior of top managers and their ability to communicate culture effectively are the biggest determinants of ethical behavior among employees. If top managers aren't willing to execute your goals and work ethic, then how can you expect employees under them to do so. Examples of unacceptable behavior include:

Gossip. Rumors can be as disruptive to a company as a hurricane. A lack of information can start rumors; frank explanations can usually stop them. However, some employees thrive on the admiration of others when they seem to be "in the know." Define gossip as clearly as you can and let employees know what you expect them to do when they hear some.

Violence or threatening or abusive behavior. Termination should be immediate for abuse of employees by supervisors or peers. This behavior only escalates with time, and is never excusable. Put employees involved on a paid leave of absence for a few days while you use the time to investigate the situation and consult with your attorney.

Dishonesty and theft. This includes theft of time, office supplies and the use of office equipment for personal projects. Set standards for what is acceptable use of company assets. Remind employees that all e-mail is considered as company business and that it is not private correspondence.

I fired members of my accounting staff for what may seem to be petty reasons: one for using $5 of petty cash as personal lunch money, another for telling me he was home sick when he was out of state on a long weekend's vacation. If key staff are dishonest at all, how can you be sure they will tell the truth when it counts?

Substance abuse. Call your attorney to make certain you follow any FDA requirements. Substance abuse is more rampant than most employers know. Illegal drugs are expensive and have led financially desperate employees to commit fraud. They have also been implicated in violent behavior in the workplace.

Human Resource Administration

The administrative portion of the human resources function can often be done most cost effectively by outsourcing it to specialists. Outsourcing can be done effectively for writing and updating employee handbooks, designing compensation programs, administering employee surveys and administrating benefits (including creating benefit statements) and in providing training for many types of skills.

Employee handbooks are probably essential for companies with more than a dozen employees. Make sure they reflect your culture and aren't a cold introduction of rules and procedures. Rules should only make work easier or create a cultural accountability. Don't expect them to cover every situation. Our handbook always included expectations, not only rules. The handbook must be updated annually to keep legal requirements current. When a handbook is introduced or updated, it should be carefully explained at employee-wide meetings. Drafting of new policies can and should be a highly participative process in order to allow employees the opportunity to think through what kind of behavior and expectations they want to have of each other. Also, be sure that you are personally willing to live with every policy in your handbook.

One of the most important provisions of the handbook should state that employment is *at will*. Specifically state that employment can be terminated at any time without cause, and that nothing in the handbook should be construed to be a contract of employment. This action will help you immeasurably when it comes to firing an employee.

Which brings us to an important point. Don't let avoiding lawsuits become more important than running your business. An ounce of prevention is certainly true here, but despite good efforts, lawsuits happen to the best of companies. Just don't allow it to become your sole purpose to see that the employee doesn't win. Keep focused on your business, and let the attorneys deal with lawsuits as much as possible.

The Bottom Line

There isn't a more important management function than working with people. There also isn't a much bigger risk your company takes on than when it is hiring a new employee. Give human resource matters the planning and time they deserve. Decide to treat employees fairly, but also commit to spending most of your time with employees who can grow to be outstanding members of your team. Spend as little time as possible with discipline problems; help departing employees leave in a gracious and honest manner.

Provide the best benefits you can, but remember, what your employees want most from you is free: the benefit of your wisdom and expertise to help them grow in their careers and your recognition of their accomplishments.

Get the support you need to deal with the people issues. Find other business professionals you trust to call and discuss problems for which you may need outside perspective to solve. Although you may be tempted to procrastinate, act quickly when you make decisions about people, and get on with running your business.

Ask Yourself:

☐ Do you spend enough time ensuring you are hiring for the long run?

☐ Do you have written policies as required?

☐ Are you following procedures that are most likely to keep you out of employee lawsuits?

☐ Does your compensation and benefit structure allow you to hire highly-talented employees?

☐ Are your employees overworked? Do you spend a lot in overtime and temporary help? Is that number increasing?

☐ Do you tolerate gossip or other behavior that undermines employee morale?

☐ Do you ask employees to review the company?

☐ Do you give enough feedback to employees regarding their performance? Do you review them individually at least annually?

☐ Do you insist that your employees stay employable?

Annual Performance Review   (Part A)

The annual performance review process should be completed in two parts. Part A is a feedback mechanism from the employee to the manager. It is important for the manager and employee to share a dialog over the issues; both looking at the behavior of the employee alone and within the larger context of the corporate culture.

It is important to know up front what the employee thinks leads to higher productivity within the culture, and what causes obstacles to the employee's best work.

I think that it is vital to begin the process with an open mind, willing to listen to the needs and problems of the employee. The employee is likely to be forthcoming and identify his own individual inadequacies if the manager opens a discussion. Typically, the manager starts by addressing the organization's inadequate support of the employee.

Give or e-mail the employee the worksheet on the following page to fill out about a month before the annual performance is due. Give the employee at least 10 days to fill it out, but provide a date when you expect to have it returned. Set a date for your meeting together at the time the form is returned, giving yourself a few days to read the employee's responses and consider thoughtfully how this compares to your view of the progress of this employee. You can also use this time to do something about the problems the employee hopes will be addressed.

Ask Yourself:

- ☐ Is the company generally supportive of employees who are honestly trying to do their best work?

- ☐ Are there a number of employees giving you similar feedback about the company?

- ☐ Do the comments reflect a positive feeling about the company, even if many problems are listed, or are there still things that seem to be left unsaid?

- ☐ Would you agree with the employee's assessments? Are there things you can do immediately to show you are committed to that employee's success?

- ☐ Is your reaction defensive? Do you discount the employee's opinion before you have investigated the concerns? If yes, why?

Annual Performance Review (Part A)

TO:

FROM:

It is time to schedule our annual performance review meeting sometime during the next month. Please fill out this form as completely as you can and return it to me by _____. It will help me to help you. We will schedule a time to meet as soon as possible after you return this form.

What could I do to make your work more productive?

What equipment or training do you need but don't have in order to do your best work?

What could the company change (or add or delete) that would help you do your work better?

What skills and abilities do you have that you think are underutilized?

Any other comments or opinions you would like to express?

Annual Performance Review   (Part B)

The second part of the performance review process is a subjective analysis on the part of the manager regarding the various aspects of the employee's work performance. It covers the employee's specific job responsibilities, the quality and quantity of the work done, and how he or she interacts with others.

Get away from the office or at least find a place where you won't be disturbed. This is where you'll fill in the worksheet yourself, and later, meet with the employee. Set up criteria for each of the possible scores of 1-10, based on your own expectations of your whole employee group. When filling in an individual's review worksheet, consider looking back at others you have done to help maintain consistency. Also, if you have reviewed this employee previously, look back to see in what areas there have been improvement. In the comments section, in a few words, list specific incidences to illustrate the employee's behavior.

Fill in the employee's top five job responsibilities, then rate each category 1-10, adding comments where you have something to say. List the employee's star moments on the bottom of the second page, plus areas where further training or improvement are needed or wanted.

After the review meeting, you will ask the employee to take a copy of the worksheet and in the middle of the second page, write objectives for the coming year, based on key success factors, company objectives and the department objectives you have identified. It is important that you both agree on these objectives, and that you meet at least quarterly to discuss these and any other areas you signaled where improvement was required.

Ask Yourself:

☐ Can you objectively review your employees? Do you have favorites for reasons other than their work performance?

☐ Do your employees have a sense of your vision for them and their work?

Annual Performance Review (Part B)

Name _____   Date _____

Job Responsibilities	1-10	Comments

Quality of Work	1-10	Comments
1. Technical skills		
2. Accuracy, little supervision required		
3. Creativity/originality of work		
4. Communication skills		
5. New approaches to problems		
6. Accepts responsibility, takes initative for action		
7. Forward-thinking/moving in same direction as company		
8. Continues to learn and improve		

Quantity of Work	1-10	Comments
1. Meets deadlines		
2. Consistently hard worker		
3. Planning/time management/ workspace organization		
4. Does fair share of department's work		
5. Is in on time, on time to meetings and doesn't miss a lot of work		

People Issues/Teamwork	1-10	Comments
1. Solves people problems directly		
2. Positive influence on coworker morale		
3. Working relationships inside company		
4. Leadership in company/shares information and suggestions with others		
5. Working relationships outside company with customers or vendors		
6. Participates in meetings		

KSF*	CO OBJ**	DEPT OBJ***	Individual Objectives:

Outstanding Accomplishments/Qualities

Areas for Improvement/Development

*Key Success Factor
**Company Objectives
***Department Objectives

☐ Do you have the courage and organizational support to be honest with your employees about their work performance?

☐ Do you spend at least 90 minutes preparing for an employee review meeting, and at least 90 minutes meeting with the employee?

☐ Are review sessions a productive meeting of the minds? Or are they 1) Angry and defensive, or 2) Just a gloss over the real problems?

Team Feedback

This is another part of the total 360-degree review process. A 360-degree performance review is intended to give an employee a full circle of feedback from everyone that the employee works with on the job.

A caveat: there must be adequate preparation for a company to launch into this process. People who have never received completely honest reviews from their supervisors and have not had an opportunity to personally evaluate their own strengths and weaknesses are not ready to hear brutally honest comments from their peers and others. Training with case studies and role playing should be required in order to give employees both a sense of how to give helpful, constructive and practical feedback as well as how to personally accept such feedback.

The review forms that will be used to solicit feedback should be given to employees three to six months before the actual process. This isn't a surprise inspection—if employees know what standards will be used to measure them, they will begin to change their behavior immediately so as to not receive negative reviews. If handled this way, you will begin to get the desired result before you even ask for feedback from peers. After all, wouldn't the best result be uniformly positive feedback from happy coworkers?

This form should be given by the supervisor to a representative number of people who are in a position to review this employee's work. If the coworker reports to the same manager, then he or she is considered a team member. If the coworker reports to another manager, the coworker would be considered a peer. I suggest doing this process twice the first year in order to give an employee an opportunity to raise his score quickly. The first time this feedback review is given is the time the scores are usually the lowest.

When all worksheets are returned, the supervisor should tally an average score by adding up the total of the 1-10 scores by question and dividing that number by the number of people who answered the question. Comments should be collected on another sheet by the question number.

The supervisor should meet with the employee to discuss the team feedback results. All feedback should be given confidentially. A total average score for all questions of 7 or above should be considered excellent. The goal of the meeting should be to look for five items that the employee would like to impact before the next review. A strategy for training, development or more individual feedback (such as individual testing or coaching) should be created for that employee.

Ask Yourself:

☐ Do you agree with the feedback given by team members and peers to the employee? Can you help coach her to better her performance?

☐ Are you willing to commit to the time it will take to make a 360-degree feedback process successful in your company?

☐ Have you trained employees to know how to give and receive feedback?

☐ Do you know what characteristics you are looking for in top level employees? Does this process help you measure for that?

☐ Are you willing to participate in a 360-degree feedback process yourself? Are you committed to your own development?

Team Feedback

Please circle your relationship to

_____ (name)

Team member   Peer   Return this form to _____(supervisor)
by _____ (date).
Please rate his or her performance in the following categories. 10= best
Your scores and comments will be kept confidential.

Quality of Work	1-10	Comments
1. Technical skills		
2. Accuracy, little supervision required		
3. Creativity/originality of work		
4. Communication skills		
5. New approaches to problems		
6. Accepts responsibility, takes initiative for action		
7. Forward-thinking/moving in same direction as company		
8. Continues to learn and improve		

Quantity of Work	1-10	Comments
1. Meets deadlines		
2. Consistently hard worker		
3. Planning/ time management/ workspace organization		
4. Does fair share of department's work		
5. Is in on time, on time to meetings and doesn't miss a lot of work		

People Issues/Teamwork	1-10	Comments
1. Solves people problems directly		
2. Positive influence on coworker morale		
3. Working relationships inside company		
4. Leadership in company/shares information and suggestions with others		
5. Working relationships outside company with customers or vendors		
6. Participates in meetings		

Comments:

Management Skills Feedback

The worksheet in the pages that follow intend to give feedback to managers on their performance, specifically their people management skills.

Although managers are required to give feedback to employees, they may be reticent to get it themselves. While employee performance problems can hurt a company, key manager problems can kill it. It is imperative that managers know that employees will have the opportunity to communicate with senior executives or even the Board of Directors, confidentially.

A company should not attempt to start a 360-degree review process unless all levels of employees are willing to participate equally. Again, managers should know at least three to six months in advance that their performance will be reviewed by their subordinates. This kind of process can bring issues to light such as possible sexual harassment or favoritism.

Have all subordinates fill in these forms and return them to a senior manager. They should be tallied with an average score per question by adding up the total of the 1-10 scores and dividing that number by the number of people who answered the question. Comments should be collected on another sheet by question number.

A senior executive should meet with the manager to discuss the feedback results. It is imperative that all feedback be received confidentially without references that would allow the manager to guess the identity of the giver of a particular type of feedback. The intent is the personal and professional growth of the manager, not the opportunity to punish subordinates for their honesty.

An average total score of 7 or above should be considered excellent. The goal of the meeting should be to select five items the manager would like to positively impact before the next review. The company should be willing to provide the resources necessary to make this a priority (individual personality testing, outside coaching) and to create a plan for development.

Ask Yourself:

☐   Are managers trained well enough to give and accept feedback?

☐   Are managers committed to their own development or do they feel they must be unquestionably "right" to lead effectively?

☐   Do managers see this process as integral to promotional opportunities?

☐   Are sufficient resources available to employees who want to get the most out of this process—outside coaches, mentors, psychologists, personality and skills testing, training programs for job skills and people skills?

☐   Is your company paying lip-service to professional development or is it an integral part of your quality program?

Go to worksheet on the following page   →

Management Skills Feedback

Please rate your supervisor's/manager's performance in the following categories.
1-10, 10=best/yes. Your scores and comments will be kept confidential. Please
return to _____ by _____.

Communication	1-10	Comments
Makes himself or herself available for communication		
Is able to communicate honestly		
Has given me wise suggestions about work or people		
Is able to gracefully handle my communications		
Treats people equally		
Planning		
Is an effective manager		
Shows signs of stress much of the time		
Can plan group workload effectively		
Performance		
Sets appropriate goals for the group		
Distributes work fairly in our group		
Sets accountability standards fairly		
Holds people accountable consistently and fairly		
Recommends appropriate compensation		
Feedback		
Gives constructive feedback		
Controls anger/is not abusive		
Recognizes outstanding achievement		
Gives credit to others		

Leadership	1-10	Comments
I respect this person		
A good example as a role model for our corporate culture		
Doesn't gossip or allow other behavior that undermines morale		
Seems happy to be at this company		
Carries out company rules and supports company policies		

Other comments you wish to make about your supervisor/manager or about his or her leadership style?

Employee Ranking System

This worksheet is intended to be used by each department manager confidentially as a human resource management tool. It is a place for each manager to record his thinking about individual employee performance of those making up his team.

It is important that a time be set aside for managers to discuss their employee-related problems, even if they don't share individual scores. Managers should provide confidential support and feedback for each other in dealing with these critical but challenging management issues.

Put each employee's initials across the top row of boxes in the worksheet. Then rank each employee from 1-10 on each of the dimensions down the left column. At the bottom of each column, total each 1-10 score, and divide by the number of categories for an average score. This is just a thumbnail sketch of each of your employees, but the bottom average should give you an indication of who your top performers are and who are the weaker links in the chain.

Look at your scoring this way: scores of 8-10 indicate your strongest employees. Make sure you are spending enough time mentoring these employees who have the potential to become your next leaders. Most employees will probably fall in the 5-7 category, and will need a variety of developmental plans.

Employees with overall scores of 4 or under have come to a critical point. Can they move up within the next two to three months to a 5 or better? If not, you should make the decision to let them go or move them into jobs that better suit them. Once you have made this decision, you should let these employees know as soon as possible and do what you can to ease their transition.

Ask Yourself:

☐   Are most of your employees in the 6-10 range? Are you prepared to take action on employees with lower scores?

☐ Do you find more performance problems in one category than in others? Are they people problems that could be solved by training? Quality or quantity problems that might be due to work overload or inadequate resources?

☐ Are lower scores due to lack of skills, a lack of interest or a lack of willingness to perform up to capacity?

☐ Are you looking for promotional or other leadership opportunities for employees scoring in the 8-10 range?

☐ Are a few much lower scores bringing down the average for particular employees? Can you give these individuals honest feedback to help them improve these scores?

Go to worksheet on the following page　　→

Employee Ranking System (by Department)
1-10, 10=best

Quality of Work (use employee initials)							
1. Technical skills							
2. Accuracy, little supervision required							
3. Creativity/originality of work							
4. Communication skills							
5. New approaches to problems							
6. Accepts responsibility, takes initiative for action							
7. Forward-thinking/moving in same direction as company							
8. Continues to learn and improve							

Quantity of Work							
1. Meets deadlines							
2. Consistently hard worker							
3. Planning/time management/ workspace organization							
4. Does fair share of department's work							
5. Is on time, rarely absent							

People Issues/Teamwork							
1. Solves people problems directly							
2. Positive influence on coworker morale							
3. Working relationships inside company							

4. Leadership in company/shares information and suggestions with others								
5. Working relationships outside company with customers/vendors								
6. Participates in meetings								
Total (A)								
Number of categories (B)								
Overall Rank (A/B)								

Employee Profile

The purpose of this worksheet is to initiate the sharing of information between employees. It can be done on paper, but is much more effective if it is available on the company's network or intranet.

Employees should think of each other not as competitors, but as the valuable resources they are. The more they think of each other as colleagues with a variety of skills, the more likely they are to call on each other for help and guidance. This worksheet will also help new employees learn where to go for help and generally who does what, making them productive that much sooner.

The idea is that when task forces are needed across departments, the manager can look for employees with special skills and backgrounds in projects similar to the one of the current task force.

Ask each employee to fill out this worksheet as completely as possible. It is important that it is kept up-to-date in order for it to be maximally useful to others. Other items pertinent to your company could and should be added.

Ask Yourself:

☐　What special skills do your employees possess that are underutilized at the company?

☐　Could these sets of profiles suggest a restructuring of departments or of project leadership?

☐　Could these worksheets also be used with supplier contacts or other independent contractors or freelancers who you often use as resources?

☐　Would a similar profile be helpful to have from members of the Board of Directors?

☐　Do you have a mechanism for ensuring that profiles are kept up-to-date?

Employee Profile

Name:
Position Title:

Department:
Phone number/extension:
e-mail:
Fax:
Hours and Days in Office:
Best time to call:
Vacation time planned:

Annual Goals

Current Projects

Special Skills

See me if you need help with:

Bio *(include professional degrees/designations, prior experience and background, publications or patents)*

Employee Opinion Survey

This is a traditional opinion survey, meant to be used at about the same time each year and trended over time. Add questions as they seem pertinent to particular items of concern.

Ask employees to fill this out and return it via e-mail or on paper. It can be done anonymously. Tally a score for each question by adding up the total 1-10 scores and dividing by the number of responses back with that question answered. Congratulate yourselves on scores of 8-10. Plan to work throughout the year to increase scores of 5-7. Items scored 4 or below must be considered high priority items and task forces should be considered to find solutions immediately.

Always give employees feedback about overall scores as soon as possible—at least within two weeks. Keep comments grouped by type on a separate sheet. Respond to those who ask for a personal response by letter or meeting within two weeks as well.

Ask Yourself:

☐ Rank your problem areas by type in the survey. Are they what you expected?

☐ Are there steps you can take to immediately show your concern for employees and their concerns?

☐ Are long-term problems such as an unworkable facility or inadequate benefits being dealt with? Are employees aware of the progress?

☐ Are employees generally upbeat about the company?

☐ Has employee morale gone up or down over time?

Employee Opinion Survey

Directions: Please read the following statements and respond with the number that is closest to your opinion or attitude. 10= strongly agree; 5= have no opinion; 1=strongly disagree

Return to _____ by _____.

Physical Facilities

1. For my area, the lighting, ventilation and general working conditions are very good. _____
2. Other than my own computer, the supplies and machines I use are very good. _____
3. The computer hardware and software fill my needs very well. _____
4. Safety conditions here are very good. _____
5. My work space (desk, etc.) provides me with a lot of room to work. _____

Compensation/ Benefits

6. For what I do, the pay is fair. _____
7. The reasons for getting or not getting a raise are very clear. _____
8. My pay here is higher than if I work at another organization. _____
9. The insurance benefits are as good as other organizations. _____
10. I have a clear understanding of all the benefits the company provides. _____

My Job/ Supervisor

11. My on-the-job training has been very good. _____
12. The instructions that my supervisor gives me are always clear. _____
13. The amount of freedom I have to do a good job is all I need. _____
14. My last performance review with my supervisor was very helpful and informative. _____
15. I think I am supervised not too closely, but just about right. _____
16. The amount of feedback our department gets as to how we're doing is very good. _____
17. I always know what my supervisor expects from me. _____
18. I always feel secure in telling my supervisor what I think. _____
19. My supervisor has pets and favorites. _____
20. When handling discipline, my supervisor is always fair. _____

Business Plans to Game Plans

21. My supervisor handles my complaints and problems very well. _____
22. I am never unfairly criticized by my supervisor. _____
23. The amount of work expected of me is considerable, but within reason. _____
24. My supervisor always gives me credit for a good job when I do one. _____
25. Overall, my supervisor always does his/her job. _____

Company Climate/Teamwork/Future

26. I find my work satisfying. _____
27. If I do good work, my job is secure. _____
28. The people I work with get along well together. _____
29. There is not enough cooperation between my department and other departments. _____
30. I have pride in our organization. _____
31. If a good friend should ask me about a job here, I would strongly urge him/her to work here. _____
32. For those who want to, there are opportunities to get ahead. _____
33. I think my future here is very bright and secure. _____
34. Employees are fairly selected for promotion. _____
35. I can trust top management to be fair. _____
36. The opportunities to talk to management, other than my supervisor, are many. _____
37. Top management seems to enforce company rules and policies appropriately. _____
38. I think top management is sincerely interested in the employees. _____

Considering all the questions, the one area where I most want to see improvement is _____ (write in the number of the question).

Comments on areas that weren't covered by this survey:

Other Comments:

❑ I'd like a personal response to my survey. Name

_____

❑ I'd rather remain anonymous.

Company Performance Review

The purpose of this questionnaire, which takes up the next several pages, is to determine the ethical issues of concern in the corporate culture. It should be given at a different time than the Employee Opinion Survey. The Employee Opinion Survey seeks to understand employee comfort and morale. The Company Performance Review asks employees to rate behaviors that could kill a company over time if left unchecked.

All of the questions aim to address issues that have done tremendous damage to companies in the past. They all pertain to the actions of individuals that may be unknown, known or even condoned by the organization. Problems in these areas can only be solved by the CEO setting standards for acceptable work behavior. And in turn, managers must execute these standards.

This review must be anonymous or employees won't be comfortable answering honestly. The object here is to make all employees suddenly more aware that common actions within companies can do real and lasting damage. It is an effort to increase the recognition of ethical issues, thereby facilitating the setting of standards.

The directions to the following worksheet ask that employees fill out one column at a time with a single 1 or 2. The first column asks whether a particular behavior should be considered (in the employee's opinion) ethical or unethical, right or wrong. The second column asks employees whether this behavior is exhibited at the company.

The most serious problems (again, in the opinion of the employee) will be those with a score of 1 in the first column and also 1 in the second. The company can assume that it doesn't need to be concerned with any questions in which scores of 2 in the first column and 2 in the second column were uniformly present.

Ask Yourself:
☐ Are there ethical issues you uncovered with this survey that surprised and concerned you?

Business Plans to Game Plans

☐ Are you satisfied that the standards of behavior you have set are high enough?

☐ Are there items that should be added to this list that are unique to your company or industry?

☐ Do you have a policy and procedures manual or employee handbook that sets standards on these issues?

☐ Should some of these behaviors be cause for termination of employment?

Company Performance Review

Please help us improve the performance of our company by taking the time to give some feedback. The first time you go through this review, please only pay attention to column 1 and write in the number 1 or the number 2, depending on how you think the behavior described should be perceived (not whether you find it here at the company). 1= this is wrong, 2= this really isn't a problem

After you have column 1 filled in with numbers, fill in column 2 by answering the question with regards to how we behave here at our company. 1= yes, 2=no

Employees. . . .	Column 1	Column 2
Don't give a full day's work for a full day's pay		
Take office supplies home		
Use the organization's telephone, fax, computer, photocopier for personal use		
Accept gifts or favors from suppliers		
Distort or falsify internal reports		
Fill out time sheets with less than 100% accuracy		
Gossip about other employees		
Pad expense reports		
Plan company-paid trips around personal needs to travel		
Use company vehicles for personal errands		
Use company letterhead for personal correspondence		
Backdate reports or other documents to make it appear they complied with procedures or completed work on time		
Say nothing when others are obviously violating rules		

Business Plans to Game Plans

Undermine morale		
Hold outside jobs that may have a conflicting interest		
Do other work on this company's time or with its equipment		
Supervisors/Managers. . . .		
Discriminate by gender or race in hiring, promotion or pay		
Abuse employees		
Deal inappropriately with ill or injured employees		
Allow or rationalize unsafe or unhealthy working conditions		
Discourage internal criticism about unfair activities		
Fail to give timely an honest performance review		
Fail to give promised salary increases		
Inadequately train employees		
Do not allow appropriate participation of qualified staff members in major policy decisions		
Have unfair work performance expectations		
Inadequately compensate employees		
Do not pay overtime for extra work		
Take credit for staff accomplishments		
Blame employees for their own mistakes		
Advance their personal career instead of working in the best interest of the organization		
Gossip about other managers		

Cast doubt on the credibility of other managers		
Create unhealthy competition between employees		
Give inadequate feedback or withhold information to gain or keep power to themselves		
Ignore company policies when they want		
Discipline unfairly or inhumanely when discipline is warranted		
Top Management. . . .		
Mismanages corporate assets		
Accepts or creates reports that distort our actual performance		
Fails to address long-term problems		
Fails to discipline or terminate incompetent managers		
Pays itself in excess of its worth		
Misallocates human resources		
Inconsistently applies policies between staff or departments		
Has conflicts of interest		
Is not living up to our mission statement		
In Terms of Customers. . . .		
We care about our customers		
We display rude or arrogant behavior to our customers		
We say unkind things about customers when they aren't there		
We provide an inadequate response to customer requests		

Business Plans to Game Plans

We make offers to customers to increase sales knowing we don't have the product available or the staff to handle the needs		
We do not make it a priority to respond to customer requests in a timely manner		

Comments:

Human Resource Key Indicator

This worksheet allows you to gauge the morale, productivity and efficiency of the workforce.

Generally, absenteeism will go up when employees are taking vacations in the summer. But, watch for a higher absenteeism within departments as a possible trend of discontentment.

If you have staffed correctly, temporary labor and overtime should be zero most months, or reflect your seasonality. An increase two months in a row could indicate a more regular need that should be filled. Because overtime pay is higher than regular pay, some employees will find reasons to work extra hours. All overtime requests should be approved in advance to keep this extra premium to a minimum.

Tracking trends and asking the right questions should let employees know that you are watching this expense carefully.

I also track the number of suggestions in the suggestion box as a general indicator of morale problems. If you see a sudden increase, consider it a sign for concern and take steps such as an employee survey to determine the reasons.

List, for each department, the number of days missed due to the variety of reasons listed, and get the average days missed per employee by dividing the total days missed by the number of employees.

Also determine the amount of money spent on overtime and temporary help by entering the number of hours worked and multiplying by the rate per hour.

If you use a suggestion box, tally the number of suggestions and attach them to this worksheet.

Human Resource Key Indicators
for _____
(month/year)

Absenteeism (# of days missed this month):

Department	Vacation	Sick Leave	Personal Leave	Total	# of Employees	Average/ Employee

Overtime:

Department	# of Hours	Overtime Premium	$	Total $

Temporary Labor:

Department	# of Hours	$ Rate/Hours	Total $

Attached: ☐ number of suggestions from Suggestion Box (attached)

Ask Yourself:

☐ Are employees in certain departments taking more time off than those in others? Does this suggest anything about the type of work or management that goes on in different departments?

☐ Are some departments making up for lost time with overtime or temporary help?

☐ Can efficiency be increased to reduce the need for overtime or temporary labor?

☐ Are there specific, meaningful connections between fluctuations in human resources indicators and spikes in inventory or order backlogs? If so, what can you do to smooth out these spikes?

Business Plans to Game Plans

Conclusion:

Winning the Game

It's hard for me to imagine this now, but before I became CEO I felt no direct connection to the financial well-being of the company. As a writer, I took pride in the quality of my work. I believed that my skills added value to the company. I felt that my coworkers liked me and respected me. But I let other people—more inclined for that kind of work—take care of the business end of things. My bonus aside, it didn't occur to me to ask about the financials; my job description said nothing about making money. Nor would I have been interested enough to ask what our financials meant had I seen them.

In short, since I didn't understand the financial end of the business, I couldn't see how my job connected to the work done in the accounting department. I considered those coworkers as dependable people, but I didn't try to understand what they did behind their computers all day. What was important to me was that I could depend on them to get my paycheck out on time.

Occasionally, at staff meetings, the CFO would ask us to hold down our spending. But this had little effect on my behavior, since the people in my department spent money only on the occasional visit to clients or to attend seminars.

As for the marketing department, we always grumbled that it spent too much money. And as long as operations got our books printed and shipped on time, I was happy.

The Value of Persistence

In all, like many employees, I had no appreciation of what it takes to run a company. But I had always believed in the ability of people to do just about anything. I believed in business as a force for good in the world, and in the capacity—indeed, the desire—of ordinary people to find meaning in the activity of business and contribute to society.

I came to the position of CEO with an advantage in building a game plan: I thought all the other employees were just like me—smart, but uninformed. Ready to learn, but with no available teachers. For years we had all second guessed management decisions; now we were calling on ourselves to make the important decisions.

And when I became president of my company, I discovered that, like me, those who worked with me believed that we could turn a sleepy little company into a lean performer, poised for growth. With the help of the ideas put forth in this book, we accomplished that goal. And now, because we enjoyed the hard work as much as the accomplishment, I have had the opportunity to share the essentials of how we came to our goal.

There have been many iterations of the formulas and worksheets in this book. And I'm sure there will be many more as time goes on. But they do articulate the central argument of this book: a good business plan deserves to be implemented well, and that any reasonably bright person with enough commitment and concentration can make it happen.

The Challenge of Participative Management

A caveat: if you choose the path of including your employees in the management of the company, you will be doing something for which little precedent exists. You will find little in management literature to support or guide you in the difficulties you will encounter. Despite a host of experts who talk about empowerment, few practical models exist.

Empowerment should mean imparting the wisdom and sharing the tools you need to perform a job successfully. But in doing so, you may be giving employees more responsibility than they want. I've asked myself the following questions:

- ☐ By giving more decision-making responsibility to employees, are you avoiding your responsibility for managing the company—and isn't that your job, not theirs?

- ☐ Are you passing the buck to your employees for decision-making? Are less capable, informed and trained people making decisions?

- ☐ Is decision-making too decentralized? Do you end up with "decision by committee?"

- ☐ Are you making peoples' lives more complicated and more difficult? Are you creating chaos instead of clarity?

The answer isn't clear, but in struggling with these issues I allowed employees to struggle with their own problems. I wanted to create an environment with minimal rules, lots of open communication and sharing of information and high quality thinking.

Challenges Met and Challenges to Come

Celebrate your successes as a group and jointly take responsibility for your defeats. Watch the scoreboard and give your people reason to watch, too. Keep your operations simple and strong. Do this, and you'll win with a properly executed game plan.

It worked for us. In 1996, Merritt Publishing became a 100 percent employee-owned company. But this was not the end of the game—new challenges immediately confronted us that meant, once again, a reevaluation of who we were and where we wanted to go. It meant a new business plan and a new game plan.

Business Plans to Game Plans

In 1998, the employees voted almost unanimously to sell the company to a larger, computer-based training company. My employees believed in their abilities and wanted to participate as a player in the Internet market. Many share an ambition to someday start and run a company. These people will undoubtedly deal with similar challenges, opportunities for growth and people management. I hope this book will help them develop new business plans and new game plans.

Appendix One:

Drafting the Successful Business Plan

A well-written business plan is critical. The worksheets in this book can be integral to your planning and then to the implementation of your plan. Use the worksheets in this book as the base for your initial plan or to do annual planning work as well.

Sections of the Business Plan	Worksheet	Page
I. Executive Summary	Vision Statement	39
	Mission Statement	42
II. Product/Service and Industry Analysis	Industry Questionnaire	192
	Assessment of Competition	195
	Product Development Proposal	204
	Product Development Sales and Cost Forecast	209
III. Market/Target Customer	Product Sales by Customer	226
IV. Marketing Strategy	Product Sales by Marketing Method	200

V. Business Objectives	SWOT Analysis	48
	Key Success Factors	52
	Dollar Sales Projections by Month	100
	Breakeven Analysis	122
VI. Management	Employee Profile (managers)	315
VII. Financial Review	Unit Sales By Product	92
	Dollar Sales Projections by Product	96
	Payroll Projections	112
	Total Company Projections	118
	Year At a Glance Income Statement	140
	Year At a Glance Balance Sheet	146
	Year At a Glance Financial Analysis	150
	Analysis of Cash Position	167
	Key Financial Indicators	169

Tips for Successful Business Plans

☐ Attempt to keep the document to a 30-page maximum.

☐ Make the executive summary easy to read and fun—this is the part that gets read.

☐ Make your financial forecasts realistic, but optimistic.

☐ The quality of your management is crucial.

☐ Product/services must be unique, but you must thoroughly describe your competition. If there is no perceived competition, there may not be a market.

☐ List any potential problems and the risks of business failure. If you can't think of any, you haven't thought this through thoroughly.

☐ Tailor the business plan to your audience. A business plan for investors is different than a business plan to be read by employees.

Business Plans to Game Plans

Appendix Two:
Creating the Annual Planning Process

Annual planning is as integral to the success of your implementation as a business plan is to getting funded.

Before the Planning Meeting: The following worksheets should be prepared in advance of your planning process or annual retreat. It is helpful to assign each participant a portion of this work and then to compile all the results in a notebook for each participant to be handed out and read in advance. Begin this process at least 60 days (preferably 90 days) before the meeting to allow for surveys outside the company to be done and tabulated.

Annual Plan/ Planning Notebook	Worksheet	Page
I. Background	Vision Statement	39
	Mission Statement	42
II. Internal Analysis	Employee Opinion Survey (results)	317
	Company Performance Review (results)	321
	Human Resource Key Indicators	326

III. External Analysis	Industry Questionnaire	192
	Assessment of Competition	195
	Customer Service Survey (results)	239
	Business Partner (Supplier) Survey	283
IV. Sales and Marketing Data	Top Selling Products	231
	Top 25 Dollar Volume Customers	229
	Customer Service Key Indicators	237
	Product Sales by Marketing Method	200
	Unit Sales By Product	92
	Dollar Sales Month by Month	222
	Product Sales by Customer	226
V. Financial Review	Year At a Glance Income Statement	140
	Budget Variance Report	154
	Year At a Glance Balance Sheet	146
	Year At a Glance Financial Analysis	150
	Analysis of Cash Position	167
	Key Financial Indicators	169

At the Planning Meeting: Use these worksheets to direct your discussion of key issues that need to be addressed so that useful plans will result.

Purpose of this session of your planning meeting	Worksheet	Page
Discuss your company's core values	SWOT Analysis	48
	Key Success Factors	52
Understand Board/Owner expectations	Owner/Board of Directors Profile	342
Work through critical issues	Critical Issues Survey	339
Set direction for next 1-3 years	Corporate Objectives	59
Establish rapport among team	Management Skills Feedback	308
	Employee Profile (management team)	315

After the Planning Meeting: Do minutes, including your corporate objectives worksheet for distribution to the rest of the staff. Set a timetable for the remainder of your planning process, which should include department and individual action plans. Create task forces to deal with critical issues.

The following are questions a company should ask itself in order to uncover its critical issues:

Critical Issues Survey

1. Do we have good cash management?

2. Do we have timely and accurate financial data to review?

3. Does the data we have help you make decisions? Do we need more? Do we look at all the data you receive each month?

4. Is our company performing well compared to industry standards?

5. Do we have adequate internal controls to prevent employee theft?

6. Do we meet with employees at least once a month to review variances and trends?

7. Are we losing market share?

8. Are overall customer complaints trending up or down?

9. Do we clearly understand our customers and markets?

10. Do we know where we are positioned in our market?

11. Are our products and services outdated?

12. Is our pricing appropriate and competitive?

13. Are we regularly creating new products and offering them to existing customers?

14. Are we satisfied with our revenue growth?

15. Are all of our product sales profitable?

16. Can we identify customers or groups of customers whose business is not profitable for us?

17. Are we satisfied with our plans to expand via the Internet?

18. Do we spend time with our direct reports, one-to-one?

19. Do we spend time with our top customers, one-to-one?

20. Are our sales and customer service people superstars?

21. Do we do self-audits on our own records, and the maintenance of equipment?

22. Do we have back up suppliers for most of our manufacturing process needs?

23. Do we have adequate internal quality controls or are our customers the first to know if one of our processes failed?

24. Are our facilities that are adequate for today also adequate for our growth plans?

25. Do we have a working just-in-time inventory system?

26. Are our facilities and information systems prepared for a natural disaster or other physically destructive force?

27. Are we making the best use of available new technologies in manufacturing?

28. Are we tailoring new operations strategies for use on the Internet or for sales via e-commerce?

29. Do we regularly chart and review operational performance?

30. Do we spend enough time to be sure we are hiring for the long run?

31. Do we have written policies as required?

32. Are we following procedures that are most likely to keep us out of employee lawsuits?

33. Does our compensation and benefit structure allow us to hire highly talented employees?

34. Are our employees overworked? Do we spend a lot in overtime and temporary help? Is that number increasing?

35. Do we tolerate gossip or other behavior that undermines employee morale?

36. Do we ask employees to review the company?

37. Do we give enough types of feedback to employees regarding their performance? Do we review them individually at least annually?

38. Do we insist our employees stay employable?

Owner/Board of Directors Profile

1. What are your desires for the company to accomplish in the years ahead?

2. Do you think the company is currently missing any opportunities it ought to be following?

3. What messages would you like to send to the staff in terms of your own philosophies about your business?

4. What would you like this planning process to accomplish for you and for the company?

5. In your estimation, what are the key internal problems facing the company right now?

6. What could really hurt the business in the next few years?

7. Do you want to incorporate any plans to change ownership into the planning process?

8. How much involvement would you like to have/plan to have in the company this year?

9. Other comments or opinions you would like to have integrated into the planning process?

APPENDIX THREE:
LIST OF RESOURCES

In choosing a list of books and Web sites that might be useful to owners and managers, I thought about what books and Web sites have both inspired me to create a participative company and what books and sites had given me good, practical advice and tools. There are wonderful free resources on the Internet and the list grows each day. Likewise, new good books are published every year.

Business Planning	**Books**
	On Becoming a Leader. Warren Bennis, 1994.
	Leadership Jazz. Max DePree, 1993.
	Visionary Leadership: Creating a Compelling Sense of Direction for Your Organization. 1995.
	The Great Game of Business. Jack Stack, 1993.
	Built to Last: Successful Habits of Visionary Companies. James C. Collins and Jerry I. Porras, 1997.
	The Mission Statement Book. Jeffrey Abrahams, 1995.

	Say It and Live It; 50 Corporate Mission Statements that Hit the Mark. Patricia Jones, 1995.
	Learning to Lead: A Workbook on Becoming a Leader. Warren G. Bennis, 1997.
	Leaders: Strategies for Taking Charge. Burt Nanus, 1997.
	The Business Owners' Basic Toolkit for Success. Joan Hartley, 1998.
	The Republic of Tea: Letters to Young Zentrepreneur. Mel Ziegler, Bill Rosenzweig, and Patricia Ziegler, 1994.
	Web Sites
	Zila.com
	Nfibonline.com
	Bizproweb.com
	Americanexpress.com/small business
	Sba.gov
	Bizplanit.com
	Sbdcnet.utsa.edu
Financial Projections	**Books**
	Budgeting Basics and Beyond. Jae K. Shim, 1994.
	Essentials of Business Budgeting. Robert G. Finney, 1995.
	Budgeting a la Carte: Essential Tools for Harried Business Managers. John A. Tracy, 1996.

	Open Book Management: The Coming Business Revolution. John F. Case, 1996.
	The Open-Book Management Field Book. John P. Schuster, 1997.
	The Business Planning Guide: Creating a Plan for Success in Your Own Business. David H. Bangs, 1998.
	The Fast Forward MBA in Business Planning for Growth. Phillip Walcoff, 1999.
	Web Sites
	Planware.org
	Moneyhunter.com
	Quicken.com
	Insweb.com
Tracking Profits and Cash	**Books**
	Counting What Counts: Turning Corporate Accountability to Competitive Advantage. Marc J. Epstein and Bill Birchard, 1999.
	How to Read a Financial Report: Wringing Vital Signs Out of the Numbers. John Tracy, 1999.
	Financial Statements: A Step by Step Guide to Understanding and Creating Financial Reports. Thomas R. Ittelson, 1998.
	Understanding Cash Flow. Franklin J. Plewa and George T. Friedlob, 1995.

	Keeping the Books. Linda Pinson and Jerry Jinnett.
	Accounting and Financial Fundamentals for Nonfinancial Executives. Robert Rachlin, 1996.
	All-in-One Business Planner. Christopher R. Malburg, 1997.
	Web Sites
	Bizstats.com
	Businessweek.com
Marketing and Product Development	**Books**
	The One-Day Marketing Plan. Roman G. Hiebing and Scott W. Cooper, 1999.
	301 Do-It-Yourself Marketing Ideas: From America's Most Innovative Small Companies. Jay Decker, 1997.
	The One to One Fieldbook: The Complete Toolkit for Implementing a 1 to 1 Marketing Program. Don Peppers and Martha Rogers, 1999.
	303 Marketing Tips. Rieva Lesonsky, 1999.
	Guerilla Marketing Excellence: The 50 Golden Rules for Small Business Success. Jay Conrad Levinson, 1993.
	Guerilla Marketing with Technology. Jay Conrad Levinson, 1997.

	The Fast Forward MBA in Marketing. Dallas Murphy, Alexander Hiam, and Charles Schewe, 1997.
	Confidential: Uncovering Your Competition's Top Business Secrets Legally and Quickly—And Protect Your Own. John A. Nolan, 1999.
	Managing Channels of Distribution, Kenneth Rolnicki, 1997.
	The Buck Starts Here. Mary A. Malloy and Michael K. Malloy, 1996.
	Achieving Planned Innovation: A Proven System for Creating Successful New Products and Services. Frank R. Bacon and Thomas W. Butler, 1998.
	The PDMA Handbook of New Product Development. Milton D. Rosenau, 1996.
	New Products Management. 5th edition, C. Merle Crawford, 1996.
	Paradigms: The Business of Discovering the Future. Joel Arthur Barker, 1993.
	Design and Marketing of New Products. Glen L. Urban and John R. Hauser, 1993.
	Achieving Competitive Edge. Harry K. Jackson, 1996.
	Innovator's Dilemma. Clayton M. Christensen, 1997.
	New Product Checklists: Proven Checklists for Developing New Products from Mission to Market. George Gruenwald, 1991.

	Power Pricing. Robert J. Dolan and Hermann Simon, 1997.
	Web Sites
	Inc.com
	Emarketer.com
	Digitalstore.com
	Entreworld.org
	Pdma.org
	Edge.lowe.org
	Hoovers.com
	Lib.umich.edu
	Uspto.gov
Sales and Customer Service	**Books**
	One to One Future: Building Relationships One Customer at a Time. Don Peppers, 1993.
	Success Leaves Clues. John Stanton and Richard George, 1999.
	Real Time: Preparing for the Age of the Never Satisfied Customer. Regis McKenna, 1999.
	Creating Customer Connections. Jack Burke, 1996.
	Enterprise One to One: Tools for Competing in the Interactive Age. Don Peppers and Martha Rogers, 1999.

	1001 Ways to Keep Customers Coming Back. Donna Greiner and Theodore B. Kinni, 1999. *301 Great Ideas for Selling Smarter.* Teri Lammers-Prior, 1998. *365 Sales Tips for Winning Business.* Anne Miller, 1998. *Building the High-Performance Sales Force.* Joe Petrone, 1999. *Sales Coaching.* Linda Richardson, 1996. *Advanced Selling Strategies.* Brian Tracy, 1996. *Seven Secrets to Successful Sales Management.* Jack D. Wilner, 1998. **Web Sites** Csmassociation.org Customercare.com Smartbiz.com Sell.org Sellingpower.com
Operations	**Books** *Breakthrough! Everything You Need to Start a Solution Revolution.* Debbe Kennedy, 1998. *Performance Drivers: The Practical Guide to Using the Balanced Scorecard.* Nils-Goran Olve, Jan Roy and Magnus Wetter, 1999.

	E-Business: Roadmap for Success. Ravi Kalakota, Marcia Robinson and Don Tapscott, 1999. *New Rules for the New Economy*. Kevin Kelly, 1997. *The Fifth Discipline Fieldbook: Strategies and Tools for Building a Learning Organization*. Peter M. Senge, 1994. *The Path of Least Resistance*. Robert Fritz and Peter M. Senge, 1999. *The Goal*. Eliyahu Goldratt and Jeff Cox, 1992. **Web Sites** Apqc.org
Human Resources	**Books** *Hiring Top Performers*. Bob Adams and Peter Verucki, 1997. *Pay for Results*. Karen Jorgensen, 1996. *Mastering Diversity*. James Walsh, 1995. *101 Sample Write-Ups for Documenting Employee Performance Problems*. Paul Falcome, 1998. *360 Degree Feedback*. Mark R. Edwards and Ann J. Ewen, 1996. *And the Winner Is...* John Leverence, 1997. *1001 Ways to Reward Employees*. Bob Nelson, 1997.

	1001 Ways to Energize Employees. Bob Nelson, 1999. *Rightful Termination.* James Walsh, 1997. **Web Sites** Toolkit.cch.com Hireprogram.com Benefitslink.com Dol.gov/elaws Workforceonline.com Bls.gov Employers.org Shrm.org
Other Resources	**Magazines** Entrepreneur.com Fastcompany.com Inc.com Successmagazine.com Businessweek.com

Business Plans to Game Plans

Index

Business Plans to Game Plans

20% Off Silver Lake Publishing books

Silver Lake features a full line of books on key topics for today's smart consumers and small businesses. Times are changing fast—find out how our books can help you stay ahead of the curve.

[   ] **Yes**. Send me **a free Silver Lake Publishing catalogue** and a 20% discount coupon toward any purchase from the catalogue.

Name:_____

Company:_____

Address:_____

City:_____ State:_____ Zip:_____

Phone:_____

Silver Lake Publishing • 2025 Hyperion Avenue • Los Angeles, CA 90027 • 1.323.663.3082

slpr

Free Trial Subscription

Silver Lake Publishing introduces **True Finance**, a monthly newsletter dedicated to money and its management. **True Finance** offers more than dry lists of mutual funds or rehashed press releases. It focuses on the trends—technological, economic, political and even criminal—that influence security and growth. It includes columns from the authors of some of Silver Lake Publishing's bestselling books, including **The Under 40 Financial Planning Guide**, **Insuring the Bottom Line** and **You Can't Cheat an Honest Man**.

[   ] **Yes**. Please send me **a free trial subscription to True Finance**.

Name:_____

Address:_____

City:_____ State:_____ Zip:_____

Phone:_____

Silver Lake Publishing • 2025 Hyperion Avenue • Los Angeles, CA 90027 • 1.323.663.3082

slps

BUSINESS REPLY MAIL

FIRST-CLASS MAIL PERMIT NO. 73996 LOS ANGELES CA

POSTAGE WILL BE PAID BY ADDRESSEE

SILVER LAKE PUBLISHING
2025 HYPERION AVE
LOS ANGELES CA 90027-9849

BUSINESS REPLY MAIL

FIRST-CLASS MAIL PERMIT NO. 73996 LOS ANGELES CA

POSTAGE WILL BE PAID BY ADDRESSEE

SILVER LAKE PUBLISHING
2025 HYPERION AVE
LOS ANGELES CA 90027-9849